LIGHT

FROM THE GREEK

NEW TESTAMENT

by

Boyce W. Blackwelder, M.A., Th.D.

BAKER BOOK HOUSE
Grand Rapids, Michigan

© 1958 by Gospel Trumpet Company
Reprinted 1976 by Baker Book House
with the permission of Warner Press

ISBN: 0-8010-0662-7

Library of Congress Catalog Card
Number: 58-8408

The author quotes from many different English translations of the New Testament. When a source is not indicated, it is from the King James Version or is the author's own translation.

PHOTOLITHOPRINTED BY CUSHING - MALLOY, INC.
ANN ARBOR, MICHIGAN, UNITED STATES OF AMERICA
1976

Foreword

Dr. Boyce W. Blackwelder's book, *Light from the Greek New Testament,* is a notable contribution toward making the marvelous truths in the New Testament more relevant and understandable to people with little or no knowledge of Greek.

It is scholarly, interesting, practical, and inspiring. Glorious new insights into God's revelation of himself through the living and written Word are everywhere apparent. It throws a searchlight on passage after passage, and reveals to most readers hitherto unknown depths of beauty and truth. This is especially true as to passages the translations of which disagree or are inadequate.

Dr. Blackwelder demonstrated his ability in scholarship and research when he wrote his Doctor of Theology dissertation on "The Causal Use of Prepositions in the Greek New Testament." And he has done so again in this volume.

—J. R. Mantey
Professor of New Testament
Northern Baptist Theological Seminary
Chicago, Illinois

Preface

Often during recent years after I have spoken at ministerial assemblies, conventions, and local churches, someone has suggested that the truths presented from the Greek New Testament be put into print and made available to the general reader. This book is the response to such recommendations.

Thought can live only if it is free to change. Though certain ideas are substantiated more and more by critical investigation, others are dispelled by the appearance of new facts. The sincere student of the Scriptures reserves the right to reconsider his conclusions when new evidence warrants that he do so. The chasm between truth and individualistic or subjective interpretation of truth is sometimes wide. The scholar tries to be as objective as possible. His supreme devotion is to truth.

The present treatise is but an approach to a tremendous wealth of data. From the mass of pertinent material, only a brief portion was considered. The investigator merely dipped here and there into the Greek New Testament, pointing out illustrative examples in a few categories of grammar and syntax.

There remains much research to be done in the vast expanses made more and more apparent as philological progress pushes back the horizons. Actually the possibilities seem practically limitless. Doubtless other writers will feel disposed to enlarge upon items herein considered and to discuss points not touched upon in this presentation. Such is to be expected in a field which offers so much by way of challenge and promise to diligent researchers.

An obligation is acknowledged to the many scholars whose writings were perused during the preparation of this volume. Full credit for all quotations and directly borrowed material is given in the footnotes and bibliography. I am grateful to the following publishers for permission to quote from their copyrighted works:

Moody Press (Chicago), Charles B. Williams' *The New Testament: A Translation in the Language of the People*, Arthur S. Way's *The Letters of St. Paul and Hebrews*, Julius R. Mantey's *Was Peter a Pope?*, and Kenneth S. Wuest's *The Practical Use of the Greek New Testament*.

The University of Chicago Press, Goodspeed's *The New Testament: An American Translation*. Central Seminary Press (Kansas City, Kansas), Dana and Sipes' *A Manual of Ecclesiology*. *The Asbury Seminarian* (Wilmore, Kentucky), Volume II, No. 2 (1947).

The Macmillan Company (New York), Dana and Mantey's *A Manual Grammar of the Greek New Testament*, Machen's *New Testament Greek for Beginners*, Chamberlain's *An Exegetical Grammar of the Greek New Testament*, and Phillips' *Letters to Young Churches*.

Harvard University Press (Cambridge, Massachusetts), The Loeb Classical Library: *The Apostolic Fathers*, Volume I; *Diodorus of Sicily*, Volume II; *Plutarch's Lives*, Volume II; *Polybius: The Histories*, Volume IV; *Josephus*, Volume IV.

William B. Eerdmans Publishing Company (Grand Rapids), Wuest's *Studies in the Vocabulary of the Greek New Testament*, and *The Gospels: An Expanded Translation;* Girdlestone's *Synonyms of the Old Testament; The Expositor's Greek Testament; The Pulpit Commentary;* and *The International Standard Bible Encylcopaedia*.

Funk and Wagnalls Company (New York), *The Preacher's Homiletic Commentary*, and Meyer's *Critical and Exegetical Handbook to the Acts of the Apostles. Journal of Biblical Literature* (Philadelphia), Volume LXX (1951).

Charles Scribner's Sons (New York), Hastings' *A Dictionary of the Bible;* and Charles's *The Revelation of St. John (The International Critical Commentary)*. The Wartburg Press (Columbus), Lenski's *The Interpretation of St. Paul's Epistle to the Romans*, and *The Interpretation of St. John's Revelation*.

Broadman Press (Nashville), Robertson's *Word Pictures in the New Testament*. Pickering and Inglis Ltd. (Glasgow), Moule's *The Epistle to the Romans*. T. and T. Clark (Edinburgh), Moulton's translation of Winer's *A Treatise on the Grammar of New Testament Greek;* and Deissmann's *Bible Studies*.

Vandenhoeck and Ruprecht (Gottingen), Heitmuller's *Im Namen Jesu*. Samuel Bagster and Sons Ltd. (London), *The English Hexapla; The Englishman's Greek New Testament;* Tyndale's *The New Testament of Our Lord and Savior Jesus Christ;* Coverdale's *The Holy Scriptures;* and Lloyd's *The Corrected English New Testament*.

Letchworth Printers Ltd. (Letchworth), T. F. and R. E. Ford's *The New Testament of Our Lord and Savior Jesus Christ* (Letchworth version). Houghton Mifflin Company (Boston), Ballantine's *The Riverside New Testament*. Sheed and Ward, Inc. (New York), Monsignor Knox's translation of the New Testament (1944).

Fleming H. Revell Company (Westwood, New Jersey), *The Twentieth*

Century New Testament. Gerrit Verkuyl, *Berkeley Version of the New Testament.* A. J. Holman Company (Philadelphia), Lamsa's *The New Testament According to the Eastern Text.*

Oxford University Press, Inc. (New York), the English Version of the New Testament (1881); and Fenton's *The New Testament in Modern English.* Revivalist Press (Cincinnati), Godbey's *Translation of the New Testament.* Follett Publishing Company (Chicago), Berry's *The Interlinear Literal Translation of the Greek New Testament.*

The Confraternity of Christian Doctrine (Washington, D.C.), the Confraternity edition of the New Testament.

Thomas Nelson and Sons (New York), the Revised Standard Version of the Bible, copyrighted 1946 and 1952 by the National Council of the Churches of Christ in the U.S.A.

The American Baptist Publication Society (Philadelphia), Helen Barrett Montgomery's *The New Testament in Modern English* (1924, 1952), and A. S. Worrell's *The New Testament* (1904).

Harper and Brothers (New York), James Moffatt's *The Bible: A New Translation,* Weymouth's *New Testament in Modern Speech,* William Whiston's *The Works of Josephus,* Deissmann's *Light from the Ancient East,* Davis' *Beginner's Grammar of the Greek New Testament,* and Robertson's *The Minister and His Greek New Testament, A Short Grammar of the Greek New Testament,* and *A Grammar of the Greek New Testament in the Light of Historical Research.*

I wish to mention the influence of Dr. Otto F. Linn, who first introduced me to the riches of New Testament Greek when I was an undergraduate student at Anderson College and Theological Seminary, Anderson, Indiana; and also that of Dr. Harold F. Hanlin, in whose classes I pursued graduate studies in the School of Religion, Butler University, Indianapolis. A special debt of gratitude is owed to Dr. Julius R. Mantey, Professor of New Testament, Northern Baptist Theological Seminary, Chicago, under whose supervision it was my privilege to do postgraduate work and to prepare my Th.D. dissertation, "The Causal Use of Prepositions in the Greek New Testament." Dr. Mantey graciously gave of his time to read the manuscript of the present work and offered valuable suggestions which I have been happy to incorporate. I mention also the help of the book editor of Warner Press and the publication committee of that organization for their assistance. But wherever errors may appear, as is almost certain in a treatise of this nature, I claim them as my own.

—Boyce W. Blackwelder

Erie, Pennsylvania
January, 1958

Contents

Abbreviations

BOOKS OF THE BIBLE

Old Testament and Apocrypha

Gen.—Genesis
Judg.—Judges
Chron.—Chronicles
Ps(s).—Psalm(s)
Prov.—Proverbs

Jer.—Jeremiah
Ezek.—Ezekiel
Hos.—Hosea
Wis. of Sol.—
   —Wisdom of Solomon
Mac.—Maccabees

New Testament

Matt.—Matthew
Rom.—Romans
Cor.—Corinthians
Gal.—Galatians
Eph.—Ephesians
Phil.—Philippians

Col.—Colossians
Thess.—Thessalonians
Tim.—Timothy
Heb.—Hebrews
Jas.—James
Pet.—Peter

Rev.—Revelation

Reference Works

D-M—Dana and Mantey, *A Manual Grammar of the Greek New Testament.*
EGT—*Expositor's Greek Testament.*
HDB—Hastings' *Dictionary of the Bible.*
R—A. T. Robertson, *A Grammar of the Greek New Testament in the Light of Historical Research.*
RSG—A. T. Robertson, *A Short Grammar of the Greek New Testament.*
RWP—A. T. Robertson, *Word Pictures in the New Testament.*
WPAP—Julius R. Mantey, *Was Peter a Pope?*
PHC—*The Preacher's Homiletic Commentary.*

Papyri

P. Oxy.—*The Oxyrhynchus Papyri.*

P. Ryl.—*Catalogue of the Greek Papyri in the John Rylands Library, Manchester.*

P. Tebt.—*The Tebtunis Papyri.*

Translations

ASV—American Standard Version of 1901.

Arendzen—The New Testament according to the Douay Version, with an introduction and notes by J. P. Arendzen.

Ballentine—Frank Schell Ballentine, *The American Bible.*

Basic—*The New Testament in Basic English.*

Berry—*The Interlinear Literal Translation of the Greek New Testament.*

Campbell-Macknight-Doddridge—Translation of the New Testament by George Campbell, James Macknight, and Philip Doddridge.

Confraternity—Confraternity edition of the New Testament.

Coverdale—Miles Coverdale, *The Holy Scriptures.*

Cranmer—Cranmer's translation of the New Testament.

Darby—John Nelson Darby's translation of the New Testament.

Davidson—Samuel Davidson's translation of the New Testament.

Englishman's—*The Englishman's Greek New Testament.*

English Revised—English revision of the New Testament (1881).

Fenton—Ferrar Fenton, *The New Testament in Modern English.*

Geneva—Genevan translation of the New Testament.

Godbey—W. B. Godbey, *Translation of the New Testament from the Original Greek.*

Goodspeed—Edgar J. Goodspeed, *The New Testament: An American Translation.*

KJV—The Authorized or King James Version of 1611.

Knox—Monsignor Ronald Knox's translation of the New Testament.

Lamsa—George M. Lamsa, *The New Testament According to the Eastern Text.*

Letchworth—Letchworth version of the New Testament.

Lloyd—*The Corrected English New Testament,* issued by Samuel Lloyd.

Moffatt—James Moffatt, *The New Testament: A New Translation.*

Montgomery—Helen Barrett Montgomery, *The New Testament in Modern English.*

Norton—Andrews Norton, *A Translation of the Gospels.*

Noyes—George R. Noyes' translation of the New Testament.

Overbury—Arthur E. Overbury's translation of the New Testament.

Phillips—J. B. Phillips, *Letters to Young Churches, The Gospels.*

RSV or Revised Standard—Revised Standard Version (1946, 1952).

Rheims—Rheims version of the New Testament.

Riverside—William G. Ballantine, *The Riverside New Testament.*

Rotherham—Joseph B. Rotherham's translation of the New Testament.

Spencer—Francis A. Spencer's translation of the New Testament.

Syriac—*The Syriac New Testament.*

Tyndale—Tyndale's translation of the New Testament.

Twentieth Century—*The Twentieth Century New Testament.*

Verkuyl—*Berkeley Version of the New Testament.* With brief footnotes by Gerrit Verkuyl.

Way—Arthur S. Way, *The Letters of St. Paul and Hebrews.*

Weymouth—Richard Francis Weymouth, *The New Testament in Modern Speech.* Weymouth-Robertson edition, revised by James Alexander Robertson. Weymouth-Hampden-Cook edition, revised by Ernest Hampden-Cook.

Wycliffe—Wycliffe's translation of the New Testament.

Williams—Charles B. Williams, *The New Testament: A Translation in the Language of the People.*

Worrell—A. S. Worrell, *The New Testament, Revised and Translated.*

CHAPTER I

Introduction

The study of language is a most fascinating and enlightening adventure. This is true especially when considering the words of divine revelation. The student who discovers something of the infinite richness they contain is rewarded for all his strenuous efforts.

Our foremost philologists have agreed in pronouncing Greek the most expressive and beautiful of all earthly languages, and of course the New Testament is the most valuable legacy to come to us from the Hellenistic age. Robertson's admirable statement on the charm of the Greek and its supreme message is appropriate here:

> The most perfect vehicle of human speech thus far devised by man is the Greek. English comes next, but Greek outranks it. The chief treasure in the Greek language is the New Testament. Homer and Thucydides and Aeschylus and Plato all take a rank below Paul and John and Luke. The cultural and spiritual worth of the Greek New Testament is beyond all computation. In the Renaissance the world woke up with the Greek Testament in its hands. It still stands before the open pages of this greatest of all books in wonder and in rapture as the pages continue to reveal God in the face of Jesus Christ.[1]

The vocabulary of the Greek New Testament is like a mighty spring, the outpourings of which no linguist can ever exhaust. It will continue to provide stimulation and challenge to future generations of readers who realize its significance as the vehicle of divine revelation. Therefore untold satisfaction may be enjoyed by individuals who study the Word of God in the original languages or who receive from the research of others a deeper and more exact rendering of the inspired message.

There is need, from time to time, for new translations of the Scriptures because all languages change and every generation needs a clear, accurate rendition of the Book of books. Certain

---

[1] A. T. Robertson, *The Minister and His Greek New Testament*, p. 28.

English words do not mean what they did a few hundred years ago; hence the proper ones must be substituted in order to express in contemporary thought the meaning of the original text.

As a result of the research and discoveries of biblical scholars, we have now a better knowledge of the Greek language and of the precise meaning of certain words and expressions of the literature of revelation. Consequently a more meaningful translation of many passages in the Greek New Testament is possible.

Obviously the translator's task is difficult. It is impossible to translate perfectly the meaning of a passage from one language into another. Much of the thought of the original can be carried over, but not all. There are idiomatic expressions, delicate shades and nuances, profound depths of truth, which translation cannot fully render. Quite often when the translator has done his best, there remains what has been called an "untranslatable residue of truth." [2] It is with this residual aspect of the biblical message that the student of the original languages works and makes his most helpful contribution.

In working with the Greek New Testament we do not disparage the many excellent English translations. All, within the limits of the accuracy possible in a translation, bring us the Word of God. Most Christians have been saved and are edified through obedience to God's Word in its translated form. We are grateful for all our reliable translations, but are eager to receive any additional insights which might be gathered from the original languages. In a treatise of this kind, we are concerned with deeper penetration into the basic doctrines of the Bible. The immutable truths of the Christian faith shine brighter and brighter in the light of evidence revealed by extensive research.

The Greek text used was mainly that of Eberhard Nestle, which is the resultant of a collation of three of the principal recensions of the Greek New Testament—those of Tischendorf, Westcott-Hort, and Bernhard Weiss. In an effort to make the word studies as helpful as possible to the person who is without the language background and specialized equipment necessary for research in the original languages, the Greek words

---

[2]Kenneth S. Wuest, *The Practical Use of the Greek New Testament*, p. 9.

treated have been transliterated. Thus the English reader may follow more easily the discussions. Quotations from the English New Testament are from the King James Version unless otherwise specified. Quotations varying from the King James, when the sources are not indicated, are the author's own translation from the Greek New Testament.

Let it not be inferred that technical scholarship alone is a sufficient prerequisite for biblical interpretation. It should be remembered that the illumination of the Holy Spirit is the basic requirement for an apprehension of truth. The student should always approach the sacred text with humility of mind and sincerity of heart, trusting the guidance of the Spirit of God. Robertson has given the timely admonition:

> We must never forget that in dealing with the words of Jesus we are dealing with things that have life and breath. That is true of all the New Testament, the most wonderful of all books of all time. One can feel the very throb of the heart of Almighty God in the New Testament if the eyes of his own heart have been enlightened by the Holy Spirit. May the Spirit of God take of the things of Christ and make them ours as we muse over the words of life that speak to us out of the New Covenant that we call the New Testament.[3]

---

[3]A. T. Robertson, *Word Pictures in the New Testament*, Vol. I, p. x.

CHAPTER II

The Language of the New Testament

Modern scholarship has exploded the once popular view that the original text of the New Testament was a peculiar kind of Greek, a religious dialect prepared under divine direction for the expression of revealed truth. The conclusion now universally accepted by philologists is that the Greek New Testament was written in the common language of the Graeco-Roman world. That is to say, the Greek of the New Testament, in all essential respects, is the vernacular Koine of the first century A.D., the *lingua franca* of the Imperial period.

The term *koinē,* transliterated from the Greek, means "common" in the sense of pertaining to the community or public at large. Hence the Koine means the language commonly spoken everywhere. It was the means of communication of peoples throughout the Roman Empire. This world speech was basically the late Attic vernacular with dialectical and provincial influences. "It was not a decaying tongue, but a virile speech admirably adapted to the service of the many peoples of the time."[1] It might be said that the period of the Koine Greek extended from about 330 B.C. until about A.D. 330.

How this universal language, such a potent medium for the diffusion of Christianity, came about is a most interesting story. The factors which led to the development of the Koine are listed by Dana and Mantey[2] as the extensive colonization of the Greeks, their sense of racial homogeneity, their national periodic religious festivals, and the mingling of representatives of the various tribes and dialects in the great army of Alexander. The result of these influences was a language common to all the Greeks. In the latter part of the fourth century B.C.,

---

[1] A. T. Robertson, "Language of the New Testament," *The International Standard Bible Encyclopaedia,* III, p. 1827.
[2] D-M, p. 7f.

the forces of Alexander the Great conquered the Medo-Persian Empire, bringing the language of the victors into the ascendancy throughout the then-known world. "Remaining as armies of occupation, and settling amongst the conquered peoples, they popularized the language, simplifying its grammatical and syntactical structure." [3]

Thus the Koine, the legacy of Alexander's conquest of the Mediterranean world, became the speech understood and used across the civilized world, making possible the proclamation of the gospel on an international scale.

Marked progress has been made in comparative philology and historical grammar since linguistic scholars discovered the nature of the original Greek of the New Testament. The strong beginning of scientific modern Greek grammar was the work of G. B. Winer whose *Neutestamentliches Sprachidiom* in 1822 inaugurated a new epoch in New Testament grammatical approach. A definite contribution was W. D. Whitney's *Sanskrit Grammar* in 1875, and there are many other distinguished names of the new era, among them Moulton, Milligan, Deissmann, W. M. Ramsay, Grenfell, Hunt, and A. T. Robertson. Robertson's monumental work, *A Grammar of the Greek New Testament in the Light of Historical Research* (1914), sums up the progress of the century and applies the new principles at salient points to the interpretation of the New Testament.

Verification of the new position is found in several areas of research. In comparatively recent years there has been unearthed in Bible lands a considerable amount of vital material which reflects many aspects of first-century life and makes possible a clearer insight into many passages of the New Testament. This important data, written in a style of Greek very similar to that of the New Testament, furnishes abundant evidence to substantiate the present view of linguistic scholars. Such authentic material from the ancient Mediterranean world offers possibilities for investigation which challenge the ingenuity of philologists. The Koine has left, in addition to the New Testament, six other literary monuments which are invaluable sources of light on the sacred text. We shall mention briefly these areas of research which are relevant to the field of biblical study.

---

[3]Kenneth S. Wuest, *Studies in the Vocabulary of the Greek New Testament*, p. 11.

Papyri

A rich source of information is the papyri—secular documents written in Koine Greek. Papyrus was the ancient form of paper. It was prepared from the papyrus plant, a tall sedge native to the Nile region. The pith of this useful plant was sliced and pressed into a writing material by the ancient Egyptians. It was prepared by arranging strips crosswise in two or three layers, soaking and gluing them together to form sheets. Then the sheets were allowed to dry, after which they were scraped with bone or shell and made ready for the pen or brush.

Papyrus was exported from Egypt to many parts of the Mediterranean world. It was used extensively for manuscripts by the ancient Egyptians, Greeks, and Romans. Some of the papyrus fragments now existing are believed to be between four thousand and five thousand years old.

It appears that papyri were offered on the market in the modern world as early as the latter part of the eighteenth century, but there were no buyers. Egyptian peasants often burned papyrus sheets for the pleasant fragrance they gave out. In the early decades of the nineteenth century papyri were again brought to the West, but did not attract much attention. Finally near the close of the nineteenth century their significance was realized, and since then papyrologists have worked upon them continuously.

Among the principal linguists in this field were the Oxford scholars, B. P. Grenfell and A. S. Hunt; the German scholar Adolf Deissmann, whose book *Light from the Ancient East* was an epoch-making work; and in England, J. H. Moulton and George Milligan, whose *Vocabulary of the Greek Testament Illustrated from the Papyri and Other Nonliterary Sources* made a major contribution to New Testament lexicography.

From the 1880's onward great quantities of papyri have been found in the sands of Egypt where the dry climate has made possible their preservation. The scrap heaps and ruins of buried cities of antiquity reveal memoranda of every imaginable sort. There are legal documents, official reports, receipts, leases, wills, marriage contracts, bills of divorce, deeds, business transactions, military records, petitions, private correspondence, accounts, invitations to dinner, references to almost every thing in the experiences of the time.

Most of the papyri discovered belong to the Koine period and give an interesting and informative insight into the life of the people. They provide thousands of examples of the language of that important era. The value of the papyri is further enhanced because the majority of them are dated and the place of writing is given. These memorials of the long ago are especially important to the student of the Greek New Testament because they exhibit the type of language in which the New Testament was originally written. In other words, the papyri show what the vocabulary of the New Testament meant in the everyday life of the people of the Graeco-Roman world. Scholars have been deeply impressed with the similarities of vocabulary, forms, and syntax between the language of the first-century papyri and that of the books of the New Testament.

The vast majority of the papyri which have come to light are written in the vernacular form of the Koine, but there are some examples of the literary Koine also. Thus these remarkable relics preserve the language of people of all degrees of learning.

Papyrological sources constitute one of the most fruitful fields of investigation, and from them comes inestimable help for the interpretation of the New Testament. Many words and expressions have flashed a fresh and deeper significance upon our understanding in the light of the papyri. Bible students owe a debt of lasting gratitude to paleographical scholars for making the results of their discoveries available for research.

Ostraca

Another valuable source of information, closely related to the papyri, is the ostraca. Earthen vessels were used universally by the peoples of antiquity, and broken fragments of such utensils could be picked up almost anywhere. The potsherd was very popular as writing material throughout the ancient Mediterranean world. Papyrus has been called the rich man's writing material and ostraca the poor man's writing material. Persons of humble means would search the rubbish heaps of their communities for discarded pieces of jars or other earthen vessels and use such fragments upon which to write memoranda of all sorts. New Testament manuscripts were few and costly, and so when the poor had opportunity they often copied Scripture portions on broken pieces of pottery.

Fortunately for scholarship the nature of ostraca is conducive to their preservation under climatic conditions which would soon destroy parchment and papyrus. Paleographers now have access to an abundance of very ancient potsherds inscribed with writing in ink. At Samaria some ostraca have been excavated, on which are short texts in ancient Hebrew, thought to have been written in Israel in the ninth century B.C. Potsherds, believed to date from the seventh century B.C., have been found inscribed in ancient Aramaic. And among Jewish texts in Aramaic of the fifth century B.C. discovered at Elephantine there are also some ostraca.

Various alphabets are represented on the ostraca discovered in Egypt, including scripts of the old Egyptian, Aramaic, Greek, Latin, Coptic, and Arabic.[4] Like the papyri preserved for us in such abundance, the ostraca are testimonials of the civilizations that long ago inhabited the Nile valley.

Of all the various kinds of ostraca discovered so far, the Greek are the most numerous. Literally thousands of potsherds inscribed with Greek have been found in Egypt, kept through the centuries in the rainless soil of that land. They illustrate the everyday Greek speech of the common people of Egypt from the time of the first Ptolemies through the Roman and Byzantine periods. On these ostraca are texts reflecting many phases of the life of the people—letters, contracts, bills, decrees, tax receipts, extracts from classical authors. The main difference between the texts on the papyri and those on the ostraca is that the latter are shorter because of the smaller size of the writing material.

The lowly potsherds were neglected or ignored for so long in the modern world because of the prevailing opinion that they were worthless. The foundation for the study of these important memorials was laid by Ulrich Wilcken whose distinguished work on *Greek Ostraca from Egypt and Nubia* opened the way for extensive work in this field. W. E. Crum, Paul M. Meyer, Pierre Jouguet, Gustave Lefebvre, and of course Adolf Deissmann are other important names in the

---

[4] Adolf Deissmann, *Light from the Ancient East*, pp. 52, 53.

history of paleography. Deissmann's *Bible Studies, Light from the Ancient East,* and other works have added much to biblical interpretation.

And so the ostraca take their place as linguistic memorials in equal rank and value with the papyri and inscriptions. They throw light upon many aspects of the age out of which came the New Testament. They furnish reliable evidence regarding the language spoken in the Hellenistic world and, of course, make a priceless contribution to New Testament syntax and lexicography.

Inscriptions

A third source of light on the Koine is inscriptions. This enlightening material dates from the period of Alexander the Great, of the fourth century B.C., to the period of Constantine, of the fourth century A.D. Inscriptions are more widely distributed than the papyri, having been found in various parts of the Graeco-Roman world "in its fullest extent, from the Rhine to the upper course of the Nile, and from the Euphrates to Britain."[5]

Most of the inscriptions are on stone, but some are on bronze and others are etched on tablets of lead, gold, or wax. Also included in the inscriptions, of which there are hundreds of thousands, are the graffiti (scribblings) found on walls, and the texts on coins and medals.[6]

Many of the papyri and the majority of inscriptions do not come from the lower classes of people, but from Caesars, generals, statesmen, and wealthy persons. The inscriptions are "usually epigraphs or notices carved upon slabs of stone for official, civic, and memorial purposes."[7]

The style of many of the inscriptions, especially those of the official kind such as legal and military documents, is more formal than that of the papyri and ostraca. However, a number of inscriptions exhibit the vernacular rather than the literary language. They often are dated, which is very helpful.

Inscriptions had been studied in the Middle Ages and in the period of the Renaissance. In the eighteenth century one

---

[5]*Ibid.,* p. 12.
[6]*Ibid.,* p. 11.
[7]D-M, p. 12.

scholar, Johann Walch, used Greek inscriptions in New Testament interpretation.[8] But Deissmann says it is the nineteenth century which should be called the age of epigraphy.

Scholars distinguished for epigraphical studies include August Bockh, Theodor Mommsen, Bishop Lightfoot, Edwin Hatch, E. L. Hicks, and Sir William M. Ramsay. Ramsay published a valuable collection of inscriptions from explorations of the ancient Christian cities of Asia Minor.

Significant contributions of immense value for biblical studies have been made by archeologists from many countries, including Germany, France, England, Austria, Belgium, Greece, and America.

The knowledge yielded by the inscriptions has been applied to the progress of New Testament philology by scholars like Theodor Zahn and Adolf Harnack, and to the philology of the Septuagint by such linguists as Heinrich Anz, Robert Helbing, and Henry St. John Thackeray. And Adolf Deissmann and H. A. A. Kennedy have shown the importance of inscriptions for early Christian lexicography. Moulton and Milligan's *Vocabulary of the Greek New Testament* made comprehensive use of inscriptions, and epigraphy wielded a notable influence in the *Grammar of New Testament Greek,* by Friedrich Blass, and in grammars by Moulton and Radermacher, and even more so in A. T. Robertson's colossal achievement, *A Grammar of the Greek New Testament in the Light of Historical Research.*

We are indebted to all the scholars who have gathered grammatical and lexical material from the inscriptions, or who have used the new texts for the compilation of grammars and various other treatises helpful for the study of Koine Greek. Books like Camden M. Cobern's *The New Archeological Discoveries and Their Bearing upon the New Testament and upon the Life and Times of the Primitive Church* give a wealth of material from the papyri and inscriptions.

Literary Koine

Another category of material of the Graeco-Roman world which is an important source of light for New Testament studies is the literary Koine. There are two types of Koine, the

---

[8]Deissmann, *op. cit.,* p. 12.

literary Koine which is represented by extrabiblical literature, by most of the inscriptions, and by a few papyri; and the vernacular Koine which is represented by most of the papyri and ostraca, by a few inscriptions, and by nearly all biblical Greek.[9]

It is not difficult to understand why there were two basic varieties within the Koine. Though no literary speech develops independently from the vernacular, yet spoken language is never identical with the literary style. The old Attic of Athens had a vernacular and a literary style that differed from each other, and such a distinction characterized the Koine from its beginning.[10]

"There was formal literary effort of considerable extent during the Koine period."[11] The forms of the literary Koine more nearly approached the classical nature of the Attic than do those of the New Testament. The Koine literati sought elegance of expression while trying to avoid pedantry. The literary Koine occupies an intermediate position between the vernacular Koine and the older classical form of the language.

Although the New Testament writers were not Atticists, neither were they "mere purveyors of slang and vulgarisms." Robertson reminds us that Paul was a man of culture as well as a man of the people, and says, "The New Testament uses the language of the people, but with a dignity, restraint and pathos far beyond the trivial nonentities in much of the papyri remains."[12] "The New Testament is mainly in the vernacular Koine, but it is the vernacular of men of great ability"[13] and reflects definite literary elements especially in the writings of Luke, the letters of Paul, and the Epistle to the Hebrews. But above all, the New Testament is the language of spirit and life.

The literary Koine is represented by the writings of Polybius, Plutarch, Lucian, Josephus, Philo, Strabo, Dionysius of Halicarnassus, Diodorus Siculus, and others. The fact that both the literary Koine and the New Testament are written within the grammatical framework of the same international Greek makes the literary works a source of information for New Testament

---

[9]D-M, p. 13.
[10]R, p. 56.
[11]D-M, p. 11.
[12]R, pp. 83, 88, 84.
[13]A. T. Robertson, Introduction to *Beginner's Grammar of the Greek New Testament*, by William Hersey Davis, p. ix.

studies. Rich rewards are gained by the student of the literary Koine, for he will discover deep insights bearing upon the vocabulary and syntax of the Greek New Testament.

The Septuagint

Among the sources of light on the Koine must be included the Septuagint, for it was written in the same style of Greek as the New Testament. The Septuagint, from the Latin *septuaginta* meaning seventy, is the most ancient version of the Old Testament. It is so called from the tradition that it was made by seventy (more exactly seventy-two) emissaries sent from Jerusalem to Alexandria for the purpose at the request of Ptolemy Philadelphus about 270 B.C. It is commonly designated by the numeral LXX.

The Septuagint was probably made for the use of the Jews who had gradually lost familiarity with their ancestral tongue as the Koine gained the ascendancy. It was the first reproduction of the Hebrew Scriptures in another language, and seems to have been the first rendition from one language into another on such an extensive scale. The Septuagint was one of the consequences of the overcoming of international barriers by the conquests of Alexander the Great and the spread of the Greek language by his victorious armies.

The structure of this important version held the respect of cultured people, and yet its language was that of everyday life. Much of the reverence formerly felt for the Hebrew original Old Testament was transferred to the Septuagint, and its common use by the Jews did much to perpetuate the type of Greek it represents. The Septuagint was the Bible of Hellenistic Jews not only in Egypt and Palestine, but also throughout western Asia and Europe.[14]

With the advent of Christianity the Septuagint was called upon to perform a new function. It became the Bible of the early church and was used extensively by the New Testament writers, the majority of their Old Testament quotations being borrowed from it. As Christianity made its way across the world, the Septuagint was a potent instrument for missionary work. It was used widely by the early Greek Fathers and was influential in molding the dogma of the Christian Era. It is

---

[14]HDB, Vol. IV, p. 437.

the version of the Old Testament cited by Philo and Josephus. Most of the versions used in the various Christian communities were made from it.

Thus the importance of the Septuagint is many-sided. It is valuable alike to the textual scholar and to the expositor, and its many contributions are appreciated by students of both the Old and the New Testaments. Of course Christianity has poured new and more significant content into many terms carried over from the Septuagint and selected from the Koine in general. Yet the Septuagint maintains an abiding importance in the field of biblical study.

Modern Greek Vernacular

The sixth source of light on the Koine is the modern Greek vernacular. Until comparatively recent times the interpretation of the New Testament Greek was almost solely in the light of Attic Greek, an approach which was sometimes inaccurate.[15]

The significant relation of modern Greek to the Koine was a discovery of the nineteenth century, dating back only to 1834 when Heilmeier first saw that the modern Greek vernacular has its roots in the Koine. Thus it became clear that modern Greek is a development from the Koine instead of from the Attic. "Vernacular is always the chief factor of change in the growth of a language."[16] The foundation of present-day Greek is the Greek of the New Testament and not the elegant language remote from the speech of everyday life. Modern Greek scholars like Hatzidakis and Professor Sophocles have done a great deal to show the connection between the Koine, the Byzantine, and the modern Greek.

The New Testament Greek exerted much influence on the Byzantine, or Middle Ages, Greek and thus on the modern Greek as a result of the universal use of the Greek New Testament. Robertson compares this influence with the effect of the King James Version on the English language and of Luther's translation of the Bible on German.[17]

So at last Byzantine and modern Greek have received the recognition they deserve. Now it is clear that modern Greek

---

[15]R, p. 22.
[16]D-M, p. 12.
[17]R, p. 46.

vernacular has unity and historical contact with the vernacular Koine and is thus part of the living stream of the New Testament speech as it has flowed across the centuries. "In general great progress has been made, and it is now possible to view the development of the New Testament idiom in the light of the modern Greek."[18] Therefore the student of the Koine may be assured that various points of grammar and syntax are made clearer in the light of the modern Greek vernacular.

Hebraisms, Aramaisms, and Latinisms

To complete at least a summary sketch of the total picture it should be mentioned that there are still other elements in the background of the language of the New Testament. In addition to Hellenistic culture, the major factor, there was the influence of the Hebrew Old Testament and of the Septuagint. Furthermore, since the New Testament writers were Jews (with the exception of Luke who was probably a Greek) and bilinguists, it is logical to expect some reflections of Aramaic, the native vernacular of Palestine.

Careful examination discloses the presence of Hebraisms and Aramaisms in the Greek New Testament, but they are far fewer than was once supposed. Comparatively there are but few. Dana and Mantey refer to examples in Matthew 19:5; Luke 1:34, 42; 20:12.[19]

The voluminous papyrus records, to which we have referred, illustrate much of the New Testament vocabulary and syntax and make it clear that many so-called Hebraisms were actually idioms of the Koine, the international language of the Graeco-Roman world.

There are traces of Latin influence in the Greek New Testament. This is to be expected inasmuch as Rome, the political power during the period in which the New Testament was written, was the concentration of Latin culture. The Roman Empire, in its many official relationships with the peoples under its control, naturally left reflections of Latin in the popular language of the early Christian period.

But the Latinisms in the New Testament are few. "The number is small, even in comparison with the Hebraisms."

---

[18]R, p. 23.
[19]D-M, p. 14.

They are mostly judicial and military terms, and "names of persons, offices, institutions,"[20] places, coins, articles of apparel, and the like.

In the light of evidence like the foregoing, the original text of the New Testament can no longer be treated as a peculiar dialect or sacred language unlike anything else on earth. Beyond any question the New Testament was written in the vernacular Koine of the first century A.D., like the speech found recorded in the inscriptions of Asia Minor and the papyri and ostraca of Egypt.

Since the turn of the twentieth century New Testament philology has undergone thorough reconstruction in the light of the evidence made available by the science of antiquities. The texts preserved on stone, papyrus, and on fragments of pottery, which have been unearthed by the thousands, present biblical scholars with a veritable storehouse of reliable information. These fascinating memorials of the Imperial period represent the ordinary language of the peoples of the Graeco-Roman world, the type of speech in which the New Testament was written. They are exceedingly valuable for the linguistic study of the biblical text both because of the wide range of their literary quality and because of their exhibition of the typical Koine. Thus by means of historical and comparative grammar the student of the Scriptures receives much aid in his interpretation of vocabulary and syntax.

---

[20]D-M, p. 15.

CHAPTER III

Importance of Grammar for Interpretation

A knowledge of grammar and syntax is a fundamental requisite for sound interpretation. A person cannot be a theologian unless he is first a grammarian. That is to say, basically exegesis is grammatical. The interpreter cannot build an abiding superstructure unless he works upon a reliable foundation. Too much emphasis, therefore, cannot be placed upon the importance of a proper beginning.

He who knows best what the vocabulary of Scripture meant to the writers who used it can best gain access to the message which those authors sought to convey. The devices and idioms of speech are of tremendous importance. Consequently, grammatical study is a responsibility of the first magnitude for man in his search for the truths of life and destiny.

The literature of the New Testament has a transcendent interest because of the nature of the communication it discloses. Each part of speech, every word and phrase, calls for thorough investigation where so much is at stake. It is the task and duty of students of the New Testament to apply the results of linguistic research to the language of this remarkable Book.

The New Testament student cannot do critical study in the purest sense until he gets back to a consideration of the text in the original language. He who knows Greek has a tool to help him toward accurate exposition of the Scriptures, and generally he is less liable to err in interpretation than he would otherwise be. When opinions of interpreters have differed widely, it has often been because a knowledge of grammatical principles was lacking. It seems that for many passages there have been almost as many different interpretations as interpreters. Thus all too often the caprice of subjectivism has given rise to strange hypotheses and vain notions. On the other hand, controversies which have raged over certain passages, where interpretation was based entirely on an English rendering, are resolved in many instances by an awareness of the significance of Greek grammar and syntax.

It should be understood that dictionaries and grammars do not determine a language; they merely interpret it more or less adequately. The supreme authority in language is not books about it, but the people who speak and write it. Usage of a word demonstrates what its meanings are, regardless of what our presuppositions may be. "The usage of the best educated writers determines the literary style of a language, while the whole people determine the vernacular." [1] Understanding of the significations of parts of speech may be clarified and augmented by considering the linguistic style of the people who use them.

The function of the grammarian is to ascertain and explain the laws of speech and to interpret properly the language idioms. By diligent study he must acquire the principles and viewpoint of the language and become familiar enough with it to handle it efficiently.

If the New Testament exegete is to interpret properly he must see the language from the Greek standpoint. If he attempts to make English, or any other language than Greek, the standard of interpretation, he will not get the idea of the Greek. "If Greek syntax is not understood as Greek, it is not truly understood." [2]

The student should realize the importance of both the deductive and the inductive methods of investigation. Deduction (reasoning from the general to the particular) and induction (reasoning from particulars to the general) complement each other and are both vital for a sound methodology. Induction and contextual analysis are very important for lexicography.

It should be remembered that words have not only root meanings, but compositional meanings, resultant meanings, and remote meanings; that their significance may be literal or figurative; and that etymology alone does not reveal the meaning of a term, but that the context must be carefully noted in order to ascertain the idea a writer had in mind.

---

[1] A. T. Robertson, *A Short Grammar of the Greek New Testament*, p. 4.
[2] RSG, p. 137.

More and more scholars have come to recognize the importance of comparative philology, the science which investigates a language in the light of the various periods of its history, and its relationship to kindred languages. "Historical grammar is essential to exegetical grammar."[3] The scientific method, therefore, is to study the language of the New Testament as a part of a greater whole, not as an isolated phenomenon. As we have emphasized, the New Testament was written within the syntactical framework of the vernacular Greek of the Koine period, hence studies in nonbiblical Koine throw light upon the sacred text.

Though the grammarian sets forth certain established principles, and his work is indispensable as the foundation of exegesis, it should be understood that he cannot solve every problem of interpretation. After he has gathered all the data he can from linguistic investigation and has made a compilation of the rules that govern the language, he must leave a large task for the exegete. For example, does Paul's expression, "the love of Christ constraineth us" (II Cor. 5:14), mean the love we have for Christ or the love Christ has for us? In such instances where grammar allows either interpretation, and where the immediate context is not decisive, it is not the grammarian but the exegete who must make the decision.

After the foregoing brief treatment of background material and principles given in Chapters II and III we look now at the text itself and consider several categories of grammar and syntax as we search for light from the Greek New Testament.

[3]*Loc. cit.*

CHAPTER IV

Nouns

The basic elements of speech are verb, noun, pronoun, and interjection. Grammarians are not sure which was the earlier, verb or noun. In the history of language probably both developed together from the same or similar roots. In reality there is not much distinction between a noun and a verb root.

The term "noun" is from the Latin *nomen,* meaning "name." Every reader is familiar with the definition of a noun as the name of a person, place, or thing. Also a noun may designate an idea, an action, or a quality. A noun is used in a sentence as the subject or object of a verb or as the object of a preposition. Any part of speech used as a noun is called a substantive.

Every category of New Testament language abounds in depths of truth which captivate the heart of the student. The various elements of speech are utilized by the inspired writers in portraying colorful and impressive word pictures. In this chapter we notice truth revealed in Greek nouns as significant vehicles of thought.

Love

Classical Greek had at least four nouns meaning "love." Various shades of meaning were expressed with the terms *erōs, storgē, philos,* and *agapē. Erōs* was associated originally with sexual passion and then came to be used of any strong affection. Eros was the name of the Greek god of love, corresponding to the Roman god Cupid. From the word *erōs* we have the English noun "erotism" and the adjective "erotic."

The Platonic use of *erōs* ennobled the word somewhat. It seemed to Plato that the intensity and strength of human passion represented most adequately the love of man's soul for higher things, and so he used *erōs* to denote the supreme human desire, that for knowledge, the chief virtue.

Erōs, in the Platonic sense denoting desire for the highest good, found its way a few times into the vocabulary of the Jews when they began to express their religious love in Greek. Examples of this more honorable use are seen in Proverbs 4: 6, and Wisdom of Solomon 8: 2. However, when *erōs* and its allied terms are used in the Septuagint, it is usually with a sensual connotation, e.g., *erastēs* meaning paramour in Ezekiel 16: 33 and Hosea 2: 5.

In the New Testament vocabulary of love, *erōs* does not appear. Though the word had religious possibilities, sexual passion was its commonly understood meaning. Inasmuch as *erōs* had the general idea of physical love, the New Testament uses other words to indicate love, and especially the love of God made known in the Christian revelation.

Although *erōs* is absent from the New Testament, it was used by some of the early Christians. Ignatius of Antioch, in his letter to the Romans, said, "My lust [*erōs*] has been crucified, and there is in me no fire of love for material things; but only water living and speaking in me, and saying to me from within, 'Come to the Father.' "[1] A little later Justin echoes the Platonic meaning of *erōs* when he says he was seized by an ardent love (*erōti*) for the prophets and Christ's friends.[2]

We sometimes find *erōs* carried over from the Greek and used in modern English to denote selfish love. In this sense *erōs* signifies the selfish interest a person may have in another person or object. Unlike Christian love, *erōs* promotes its own well-being and selfish advantage.

The distinctive meaning of *storgē* is natural affection or love for one's family or kindred. This noun is from the verb *stergō* which denotes a deep, innate sentiment peculiar to individuals who are related by the ties of nature. It expresses the delicate esteem and attention mutually rendered by those who cherish one another because of such attachment.

Storgē is the mutual love of parents and children, husband and wife, brothers and sisters, and other near relations. In a general sense *storgē* was used of any natural affection, such as esteem for ruler or country as one's own. Aristotle spoke of

[1]Ignatius to the Romans, VII. 2. *The Apostolic Fathers*, Vol. I.
[2]James Moffatt, *Love in the New Testament*, p. 38.

poets as loving (*stergontes*, plural participle) their own poems
as their children.

Storgē is the love which is characteristic of human nature
in its normal state. It signifies the noble inclinations which
spring from a genuine manly nature. The Greeks also used the
term to designate the instinctive affection or concern which an
animal has for its offspring.

Stergō and its cognates were used chiefly by classical writers.
The verb is not found in the New Testament, but the noun
storgē appears in composition. In Romans 12:10 *storgē* is
compounded with *philos* to form the adjective *philostorgos*
which means to be tenderly affectioned. Thus Paul emphasizes
the character of brotherly love (*philadelphia*). We are to treat
our fellow Christians as if they were brothers according to the
flesh.

Astorgos (*storgē* with the alpha privative prefixed, which
negates the word) is found twice in the New Testament,
Romans 1:31 and II Timothy 3:3, and is commonly translated
"without natural affection." Charles B. Williams renders it
"no human love" and "lacking in love for kinsmen"; Arthur
S. Way, in Romans 1:31, "no love for their own flesh and
blood"; J. B. Phillips, in II Timothy 3:3, "lacking in normal
human affections." *Astorgos* describes the sad state of the
calloused, inhuman person whose heart is void of the warmth
of noble sentiment for those who should be dear to him because of the ties of nature. The term was used in pagan writings to denote wives who carried on illicit love affairs. Animals
that did not cherish their young were described by this same
term.

The two common nouns for love in the Greek New Testa-
ment are *philos* (verb *phileō*) and *agapē* (verb *agapaō*). *Phileō*
is used about fifty times in its various verbal and substantival
forms, while *agapaō* appears more than three hundred times.

Phileō was used in classical Greek to express a warm affection or fondness for a person or thing. Homer used the term to
denote the love of the gods for men. It means to be fond of,
to like, to welcome, to delight in, to treat kindly, to befriend.
The noun *philos* means a friend, a companion, one who enjoys
a familiar association with a person or one who finds pleasure
in a person or object. The fondness of person for person de-

noted by *phileō* manifests itself in outward expressions, and this verb is used to signify the act of kissing (Matt. 26:48; Mark 14:44; Luke 22:47; cf. also the Septuagint, Gen. 27:26 f.).

Phileō indicates a love which has its basis in pleasure. This idea is reflected in such passages as Matthew 6:5; 23:6-7; Luke 20:46 which reveal the motive underlying the conduct of hypocrites who find pleasure in making religious overtures in order to be seen of men.

An individual loves that which is like himself, and he becomes like that to which he is devoted. Jesus says, "If you were of the world, the world would love [*phileō*, have a fondness for] its own" (John 15:19, RSV). The world loves its own because of inward kinship or consanguinity of nature. But the world finds no such affinity between itself and the Christian because the follower of Jesus has a new nature (II Cor. 5:17).

Our choices and our loves develop fixed attitudes. Thus it is that he who continues to love (*phileō*) his life shall lose it (John 12:25). He sacrifices the higher for the lower values and becomes the victim of his own subjectivism, acknowledging no objective standard of conduct, not even God himself, for he becomes his own god. The ultimate result of such a tragic attitude is vividly portrayed by John who, after describing the blessedness of the Holy City, says, "But without are the dogs [strong figure for spiritual scavengers and the morally impure], and the sorcerers, and the fornicators, and the murderers, and the idolaters, and everyone who loves [*phileō*] and practices a lie" (Rev. 22:15).

The verb *agapaō* was used by the Greeks from the time of Homer, although *phileō* was the most commonly used word for love in the classics. In the Septuagint *agapaō* translates several Hebrew terms, chiefly *ahav* which is rendered a few times by *phileō*. *Ahav*, the general term for love in the Old Testament, indicates affection, inclination, or desire, either human or divine.[3] Girdlestone says, "Occasionally the LXX adopts *phileō* instead of *agapaō*, but never where God's love is concerned."

Agapaō, which has a general connotation in the Septuagint, is used in the New Testament to designate the essential nature of God and his infinite regard for mankind. Thus *agapaō* expresses the most exalted concept of love indicated by human

[3]Robert Baker Girdlestone, *Synonyms of the Old Testament*, p. 110.

language. It denotes the new and exalted type of divine love which the Incarnation reveals. It is into the word *agapē* that the moral and ethical content of Christianity has been poured. It signifies sacrificial love which is poured out unselfishly in behalf of undeserving mankind. *Agapē* expresses that spiritual bond of love which exists between God and man and between man and man in Christ. It emphasizes divine love as the supreme, indispensable virtue of the Christian life, the foundation upon which all other godly qualities are predicated.

Agapē—unselfish, redemptive love—is the recurring theme of the New Testament. It points out that salvation is not attained by means of human culture and refinement, but is the result of the transforming power of the Christ. (Cf. Rom. 5:5.) In First Corinthians 13, the highest mountain peak in the Pauline writings, the lofty term *agapē* is used throughout. John says, "Beloved, let us continue to love [present subjunctive of *agapaō*] one another because love [*agapē*] is of God, and every one who keeps on loving [present participle of *agapaō*] is in the state of having been begotten [perfect tense] of God and knows God" (I John 4:7).

Agapaō and *phileō* were sometimes used practically synonymously in classical Greek and also in the Scriptures. For example, the Septuagint in Genesis 37:3, uses *agapaō*; in 37:4, *phileō*. In the New Testament both words are used of God's love for man (*agapaō* in John 14:23; 17:23; *phileō* in 16:27); both describe the love of the Father for the Son (*agapaō* in John 3:35; 17:23, 24; *phileō* in 5:20); both represent Jesus' love for man (*agapaō* in John 11:5; *phileō* in 11:3); and both signify the love of men for Jesus (*agapaō* in John 14:15, 21, 23, 24, 28; *phileō* in 16:27). However there is a distinction between these two terms. Thayer says that "even in some cases where they might appear to be used interchangeably the difference can still be traced."[4] As one reads the New Testament carefully he soon discovers the distinctive significance of these terms in their various contexts. Although they have a certain common area of usage, yet in general *phileō* has the idea of spontaneous affection while *agapaō* indicates a reasoning, discriminating devotion which is indicative of moral character. It is consistent

[4]Joseph Henry Thayer, *A Greek-English Lexicon of the New Testament*, p. 653.

with this distinction that *agapaō* is never used to mean "to kiss" in the New Testament.

Stone and Rock

In Koine Greek a distinction was made between *petros* and *petra,* the former being used to designate a stone and the latter to signify a large rock, a boulder, mass of rock, steep cliffs, and the like. There are illustrations of this distinction in the Septuagint. In II Maccabees 4: 41, *petros* in its plural form is used of stones small enough to be picked up and thrown by hand, while in 14: 45, *petra* is used of a steep rock upon which a man stands. Professor Mantey says, "*Petra* has the meaning of a mass or cliff of rocks, or simply of the substance which we call rock, at least fifty-two times in the Septuagint."[5] Dr. Mantey also has pointed out: "The fact that the city, Petra, southeast of Palestine, with its houses hewn out of solid rock, is so named also implies that the word was used to mean a cliff or a mass of rocks."[6]

We find similar illustrations in the literary Koine writings. Polybius uses *petra* in the sense of precipice and to signify a ridge of rock.[7] Diodorus of Sicily writes of cutting tunnels through *petra,* of numerous streams which drop from cliffs (*petra*) into the sea, of ships striking against rocks (*petra*), and of a mountain range at whose summit are rocks (*petra*) of a terrifying height.[8] Plutarch[9] uses *petra* of a cliff which is described as "huge and jagged" (Camillus, XXV.2), and of a rock upon which a heifer stood (Lucullus, XXIV.7). He speaks of a large *petros* which, however, was small enough to be picked up and thrown by a man (Aristides XVII.3). Josephus[10] says, "a river was to flow for them out of the rock" (*petra*).

In the New Testament *petra* signifies a great rock or mass of rock (e.g., Matt. 7: 24 f.; Mark 15: 46; Luke 6: 48; 8: 6, 13).

An awareness of the distinction between *petros* and *petra* clears away difficulties of interpretation in Matthew 16: 18. Some expositors, faced with a problem in verses 17-19 have questioned the genuineness of the passage. But such an ap-

---

[5]Julius R. Mantey, *Was Peter a Pope?* p. 25.
[6]*Ibid.*, p. 27.
[7]*Polybius: The Histories,* Vol. IV, Bk. X.48.5f; IX.27.4.
[8]*Diodorus Siculus,* Vol. II, Bk. III.12.5; 39.1; 40.5; 44.4.
[9]*Plutarch's Lives,* Vol. II.
[10]*Josephus: Jewish Antiquities,* Vol. IV, Bk.III.36.

proach does not come to grips with the main issue. There is no textual evidence that the verses in question are an interpolation, hence no reason for doubting their authenticity.

An understanding of the distinction generally observed in Koine Greek between *petra,* a massive rock, and *petros,* a detached rock or stone, makes the words of Jesus clear. If it be argued that Jesus probably spoke Aramaic in the conversation with Peter, and that Aramaic makes no such distinction between the terms, it can be stated that the writer of the New Testament account understood a distinction and expressed it by the two different words.

There are several strong arguments which show that Peter (*petros*) and the rock (*petra*) upon which the church is built are not identical. All the pronouns in Matthew 16:18 are emphatic, contrasting the person of Peter with the mighty rock which is the foundation of the church. The different genders (*petros,* masculine; and *petra,* feminine) emphasize a distinction in the references.

Since *petra* is used metaphorically several times to indicate Christ (Rom. 9:33; I Cor. 10:4; I Pet. 2:8), it is in harmony with the Scriptures to take it thus in Matthew 16:18. In this light Jesus means that *he* is the foundation of the church. He speaks of himself as the builder, and uses the expression "my church." So the New Testament *ekklēsia* is built upon Christ's deity and Saviorhood, upon the efficacy of his blood, and upon the immutability and objectivity of truth. It is obvious that no human being could be the support of such a structure. Paul speaks of Jesus Christ as the foundation (I Cor. 3:11).

The church is the creative work of God. Actually Peter's confession was impossible apart from the divine revelation upon which his proclamation was based. Jesus makes this point clear in Matthew 16:17. This revelation was not disclosed to Peter only. It was also the experience of the other disciples, and it is the impetus which makes possible the confession of any and all believers now as then. The church is based upon the truth which Peter confessed, that is, upon the reality that Jesus is the Christ, the Son of the living God. In verse 18 our Lord is also in effect saying to Simon, "The power of the gospel which has transformed you into a man of dependable character [implied in *petros*] will likewise change other persons, and as a result of this redemption the church is built." Thus we see that the church never produces salvation; salvation produces the church.

There is a sense in which the inspired writings and work of all the apostles and prophets have their place in the divine plan of the church of which Jesus Christ is the cornerstone (Eph. 2:20). In fact, all believers are living stones (*lithoi*) in God's temple (I Pet. 2:5). But Peter has no special position or prerogative above the other apostles. Nowhere in the New Testament is any supremacy assigned to him.

The Logos

In the prologue of the Fourth Gospel (1:1-18) John introduces the doctrine of the Logos. To arrive at an adequate interpretation of this significant idea, we must know something of the background of the term.

The noun *logos* (from the verb *legō,* to collect, put words side by side, relate, speak, say) means reason, speech, or word. It signifies not only a word in a grammatical sense, but a spoken word which implies an idea or concept. It denotes, therefore, both the thought inwardly conceived in the mind and outwardly expressed through the vehicle of language.

The logos concept had a long history, and it is an interesting study to trace the idea from its earliest appearance in antiquity through its various phases until it attained its most exalted expression in the New Testament. The development of the thought it embodies reveals the growth of man's concept of God's revelation to the world.

The term itself and the idea which it reflects were quite commonly used by the Greeks in their search for an explanation as to how Deity might come into relation with the world of time and space. It was thought that there could be no action of God upon the material universe except through intermediate agents. Heraclitus (ab. 540-475 B.C.) used *logos* to denote the universal law which maintains order in the world. Plato (427?-347 B.C.) spoke of a rational principle active in the world, to which he commonly applied the term *nous,* but he occasionally employed *logos* to describe the divine force from which the world came. The Stoics employed *logos* for the vital energy or generative will of the divine power which contains within itself the conditions and processes of all things.

In the Old Testament "the angel of the Lord" and "the wisdom of God" are expressions denoting the manifestations of Deity in his connection with the world. Other terms are used of God in his absolute being.

Philo, the Jewish immanistic theist of Alexandria (ab. 20 B.C.-A.D. 54) identified *logos* with the Wisdom of the Old Testament by which, according to Proverbs, the world came into existence. Thus in Philo Hellenistic speculation was united with Hebrew tradition to show that the Old Testament embodied all that was highest in Greek philosophy.

In the New Testament John employs the term in its highest sense by identifying the Logos with the personal Christ who makes his appearance on the field of history. The Apostle takes an expression already in use by thinkers seeking to find God's connection with the world and applies it to Jesus as the articulation of the invisible God. The ancient philosophers, as we have noted, had wrestled with the problem of divine immanence. God was thought of as infinitely perfect and holy. How could such a glorious Being communicate with imperfect humanity? Was there any means of spanning the chasm between the Perfect and the imperfect, between the Infinite and the finite? There must be a bridge whereby God could communicate with man, the Greeks reasoned, and this mystical bridge they termed the *logos* because it is by means of language that thoughts are expressed in intercourse between human minds. John applies the idea to the Christ. He says there is a bridge between God and man, and that bridge is the Jesus of history. Irrespective of the various speculations which had gathered around the term, John uses the Logos concept to express the climax of the revelation of God to man of which the earlier Greek efforts were inadequate and the Jewish theophanies only partial manifestations.

John describes the Logos in relation to God and to the world. He says, "In the beginning was the Logos" (John 1:1). The language is similar to the Hebrew *be reshith* of Genesis 1:1. In the opening verses of Genesis Moses starts his narrative with the creation of the cosmos and comes forward along the annals of time, whereas John starts at the same point and takes us backward along the measureless avenues of eternity. For John the Logos is pre-existent. The Logos did not come into existence "in the beginning." At the point at which all things began, He already *was*. The Word is before time. He is coexistent and coeternal with God the Father.

"And the Logos was with God [*pros ton theon*]." The preposition *pros* carries the idea of "face to face," and implies not merely coexistence but personal communion and thus separate personality. This is a beautiful view of the Deity of the Son, as John pictures God and the Logos on the plane of divine equality as person to person face to face with each other eternally.

"And the Logos was God." Three times in this sentence John uses *was* (*ēn,* imperfect tense of the verb *eimi,* to be) which emphasizes the fact of no origin for God or for the Logos and shows their continuous existence. A different verb (*egeneto,* became) is used in John 1:14 to denote the incarnation of the Logos.

The creative cosmic relationship of the Logos is set forth in John 1:3: "All things came into existence through him." In the following verse we are told that in Him was "life" and "light." These two terms, along with "love" (*agapē*) in First John constitute a triad expressing John's conception of the qualities which belong to the essential nature of God.

For John the Logos is both transcendent and immanent. "The Logos became flesh" (1:14), and in him is the perfect revelation of the Father. And the objective truth of the Christian faith may be verified in subjective experience, for John says, "As many as received him [Jesus], to them gave he power [*exousia,* authority, liberty of action] to become children of God" (1:12).

The Johannine delineation of the Logos concept assures us that there is above and within the total order of existence an eternity of thought and love. This means we are not here by chance. It means purpose, plan, direction. This assurance brings us peace and provides a foundation for faith, for there is an infinite, almighty hand beneath us, a Father heart to love us, a triumphant Redeemer to save us, an omniscient Guide to lead us, and an eternal goal to challenge us.

Living Creature and Beast

In rendering *zōon* and *thērion* by the same term ("beast"), the King James Version obliterated for the English reader the distinction between these two Greek words.

It is noted at a glance that the two nouns differ etymologically. *Zōon*, from the verb *zaō*, to live, is a general term which means a living being or creature, including man himself. *Thērion* is a restricted term, meaning beast or wild animal. In a metaphorical sense it signifies a ferocious, brutal individual. Thayer has pointed out that *zōon* gives prominence to the vital element of a creature, while *thērion* emphasizes the bestial element.[11]

Generally in contexts where *zōon* means otherwise than "living being," it is qualified by appropriate adjectives, e.g., *aloga zōa*, "brute beasts" (II Pet. 2:12; Jude 10). But in Hebrews 13:11 we find the genitive plural of *zōon* without any adjective, in the sense of sacrificial animals.

Throughout the Apocalypse of John *zōon* appears in contexts which indicate its meaning is "living creature" or "living being" (Rev. 4:6-9; 5:6, 8, 11, 14; 6:1, 3, 5-7; 7:11; 14:3; 15:7; 19:4), while *thērion* uniformly has the connotation of "beast" (Rev. 6:8; 11:7; 13:1-4, 11, 12, 14, 15, 17, 18; 14:9, 11; 15:2; 16:2, 10, 13; 17:3, 7, 8, 11-13, 16, 17; 19:19, 20; 20:4, 10).

The powers symbolized by *zōon* and *thērion* play significant roles in the Book of Revelation, moving in spheres which are directly opposed to each other. The *zōa* or living beings which stand before the throne of God are part of the heavenly symbolism; the *thēria*, the first beast, which ascends from the bottomless pit (11:7), and the other from the sea (13:1) constitute part of the infernal symbolism. This fact, along with the etymological distinctions, should preclude any confusion of the two terms.

An understanding of the connotations of *zōon* and *thērion* is essential for the proper interpretation of many passages in the Revelation of John. It is well that a number of translations have corrected the inaccuracies of the King James in this regard (e.g., American Standard, Montgomery, Weymouth, Moffatt, Revised Standard). But Goodspeed consistently says

---

[11]*Op. cit.*, p. 274.

"animal" for both *zōon* and *thērion* in the Revelation, thus losing the important distinction between these two words.

Along with the twenty-four elders, the *zōa* (nominative plural form) seem to symbolize the great host of persons redeemed through the blood of the Lamb, inasmuch as both the elders and the *zōa* say "our God" (Rev. 5:10).

In Josephus[12] we have the distinction between *zōon* and *thērion* as the following quotations show:

> There was a conflict of opinions: some said that Moses had fallen a victim to wild beasts (*thēriois*). . . . But the sober-minded . . . held that to die under the fangs of beasts (*thēriois*) was a human accident (Bk. III. 96, 97).
>
> This curtain was of great beauty . . . interwoven with all other designs that could lend to its adornment, save only the forms of living creatures (*zōon*) (Bk. III. 126).
>
> To the cover were affixed two figures, "cherubs" as the Hebrews call them—winged creatures [*zōa*] these, but in form unlike to any that man's eyes have seen (Bk. III. 137).

Confession

The Greek noun rendered confession (*homologia*) is a compound from *homos,* meaning "the same thing," and *legō,* "to say"; hence confession means "to say the same thing." The basic idea of the term is agreement or acknowledgment. It denotes an act which places a person in harmony with the viewpoint of another. It is the concurring in a statement previously made by someone else. The word is very common in the papyri for business agreements.

In its religious application *homologia* means that we say the same thing about ourselves that God says about us, and it emphasizes the publicity of the action. Confession in the Christian sense, therefore, means that we agree with Christ, and that we make that agreement known. We take His attitude toward sin, life, values, destiny. Jesus says, "Whosoever shall confess *in me* before men, I will also confess *in him* before my Father who is in heaven" (Matt. 10:32; cf. Luke 12:8). The phrase *en moi* (in me) indicates a sense of unity which the believer has with Christ and involves the Savior's person, his teaching, and his work. And the phrase *en autōi* (in him) is significant, for it shows Jesus' identity with the believer. Our

---

Lord is saying that if we champion his cause in this world, he will champion our cause in eternity.

The open declaration of confession implies a change of conduct on the part of the believer. It is the manifestation of an inner impulse or conviction of the heart.

In both the Old Testament and the New confession of sin before God is set forth as a condition for forgiveness, being the evidence of inward penitence and outward change. Proverbs 28:13 states a general principle, "He that covereth his sins shall not prosper: but whoso confesseth and forsaketh them shall have mercy." John reiterates this timeless truth, "If we confess our sins, he [God] is faithful and just to forgive us our sins, and to cleanse us from all unrighteousness" (I John 1:9).

The close connection between repentance and confession is seen in the results of the Baptist's preaching when many persons repented and made open confession of their sins. There is a vivid picture in Mark 1:5 and Matthew 3:6 where the present middle participle *exomologoumenoi* (preposition *ek—ex* before *vowels*—meaning "out" in combination with the verb *homologeō*) has the idea of "confessing in full," or "confessing out" their sins. We need such powerful and thorough revivals today.

In the apostolic church confession was required as an indication of true conversion and a condition for baptism. It included of course the recognition of Jesus as Lord (cf. Acts 8:37; Rom. 10:9; I Cor. 12:3).

Sometimes *homologia* is used in the New Testament to designate what is confessed, i.e., the believer's profession in its objective sense, the truth of the Christian revelation (cf. Heb. 3:1; 4:14).

For auricular confession as practiced in the medieval and Roman church, there is no authority in the Scriptures. Only God can forgive sin. Such is not the prerogative of any human minister or priest (I Tim. 2:5).

Repentance

A number of New Testament translations, including King James, American Standard, Moffatt, Montgomery, and Revised Standard, do not make a consistent distinction between the

Greek word for regret and the word for repentance, i.e., change of thought and conduct.

It is true that *metameleia* and *metanoia* were used interchangeably at times in Koine Greek with the idea of regret or remorse, apart from the sense of any violation of moral law, and that they were used likewise, though rarely, in an ethical sense. But it is also true that usage made a distinction between these terms, as might be expected from their etymological force, and the distinction is most pronounced in the New Testament.

The noun *metameleia* does not occur in the New Testament, but the verb *metamelomai* appears five times (Matt. 21:30, 32; 27:3; II Cor. 7:8; Heb. 7:21); while the noun *metanoia* is used some twenty-five times and its cognate verb *metanoeō* about thirty-five times. *Metamelomai,* to be sorry afterwards, has the idea of care, concern, or remorse because of regrettable action. It emphasizes the emotional aspect of the regret. The feeling indicated by *metamelomai* might lead to genuine repentance, or it might produce only remorse. *Metanoeō,* to think differently, signifies a change of thought reflected in conduct. It denotes a mental revolution which affects the course of one's life.

In the New Testament *metanoia* and *metanoeō* are never employed except in an ethical sense. They express that transformation of thought and life wrought by the Spirit of God in the believer.

In one passage in the New Testament, *metamelomai* seems to equal *metanoeō* (Matt. 21:30, 32) and expresses a change of thought leading to obedience. In its other appearances in the New Testament, *metamelomai* has the idea of regret but without effective change of conduct. Thus when the New Testament speaks of mere sorrow for an action, it uses *metamelomai* to which forgiveness of sins is never promised. But that genuine repentance to which remission of sins is promised is always expressed by *metanoeō*. It is significant also that *metanoeō* is often employed in the imperative mode (action commanded), but that *metamelomai* is never used in the imperative in the New Testament.

The force of *metamelomai* and *metanoeō* is clearly shown in II Corinthians 7:8-10. Paul uses *metamelomai* twice in verse 8 in the sense of regret. He uses *metanoia* in verses 9 and 10 to express the change of thought reflected in new life (repentance unto salvation, vs. 10). And he calls it salvation "not to be regretted (*ametamelēton*, negative verbal adjective from *metamelomai*). This passage makes clear the distinction between mere emotional sorrow (*lupē*) signified by *metamelomai*, and the godly sorrow (*hē kata theon lupē*) which produces genuine repentance expressed by *metanoia*.

Actually, from the etymological standpoint, we do not have any one English word which adequately expresses the New Testament force of *metanoia*. "Repentance," which is commonly used to render it, means "to be sorry again" (from the Latin *repoenitet*) rather than a change of thought and purpose. But etymology alone does not determine the meaning of a word. Usage and context also enter into the picture. Usage has given "repentance" a strong connotation in modern English, so that its meaning approximates the idea signified by *metanoia*.

In the light of the New Testament force of *metanoeō* as compared with *metamelomai*, the distinction should be maintained in translation. If both words are rendered by "repent," a qualifying term should be used when rendering *metanoeō*. There is a vast difference between regret, even if it leads to remorse, and that transformation of thought which leads to salvation. Therefore, if *metamelomai* is rendered by "repent," the rendering of *metanoeō* should be "true repentance," "genuine repentance," or the like. It is repentance which changes conduct (II Cor. 7:10) which is indicated by *metanoeō*. Another alternative, and perhaps the better one in the light of present-day usage, is to render *metamelomai* by "regret" and *metanoeō* by repent, i.e., "to amend or resolve to amend one's life as a result of contrition for one's sins" (*Webster's Collegiate Dictionary,* 1947).

From the foregoing standpoint use of the term "repent" is not entirely accurate in Matthew 27:3 (KJV, ASV, Moffatt, Montgomery, RSV) as the context shows Judas did not experience change of thought leading to salvation, but only remorse which led to suicide. Thus "remorse" is an accurate rendering of the participle of *metamelomai* in that verse (so Weymouth, Godbey, Goodspeed, Williams, J. B. Phillips).

The Fruit of the Spirit

Paul's figure of fruit for the graces of the Holy Spirit emphasizes the fact that the Christian experience is predicated upon the divine life implanted in the believer. The spiritual traits listed in Galatians 5:22-23 emanate from the presence of the Spirit of God. They are fruit, not works, and fruit grows, ripens, and comes to perfection through its relationship with the life of the vine.

The noun "fruit" (*karpos*) in Galatians 5:22 is singular, which means that the Holy Spirit reflects his presence in the Christian by the ninefold cluster of moral qualities listed. That is to say, by use of the collective noun Paul pictures a tree of spiritual fruit with nine characteristics or elements, all of which are found in a life indwelt by the Holy Spirit.

The first of the nine qualities in the cluster of the Spirit's fruit is love (*agapē*). Love is the supreme quality of the Christian life and is the foundation upon which all the other virtues are based. Not often used in pre-Christian writings, *agapē* came to be the highest and strongest word for love in the New Testament, as into this term is poured the content of the love of God revealed in the Christ. *Agapē* denotes the love which is of the essence of God. The heavenly Father gives his love to mankind, although man is not worthy. The chief ingredient of *agapē* is selflessness or self-sacrifice on behalf of the objects loved (cf. John 3:16). The *agapē* is shed forth into the believer's heart by the Holy Spirit (Rom. 5:5). See Paul's majestic delineation of the *agapē* in First Corinthians 13.

Along with love, the Spirit gives *chara*—joy, gladness. There is no human or earthly source for this elation, but it is produced by the Holy Spirit in the hearts of those who receive the word of the gospel (I Thess. 1:5-6). It begins with the experience of forgiveness and extends across the scope of time and into eternity. Thus the believer rejoices in the work of regeneration and sanctification and in the hope of everlasting glory. This is the joy of radiant optimism based on the promises of God. We are learning more and more about the influence of mental attitudes over physical life and of the importance of faith and the absence of anxiety as requisites of good health.

The word for peace (*eirēnē*, basis of the name Irene) is

probably from the verb *eirō,* to join, fasten together, hence is
a vivid word denoting harmony between individuals. It reminds
us that through the blood of the cross Jesus reunites with God
every sinner who puts his trust in the Savior. Peace is the state
of well-being enjoyed by the soul assured of its salvation
through the Christ. It is rest and tranquillity based on the
awareness of right relation to God on the grounds of faith in
the Savior. Jesus promises to his followers peace which ban-
ishes fear and worry (John 14: 27). Although this peace tran-
scends our understanding, we can experience the reality of it
(Phil. 4: 7).

The Greek word for long-suffering is *makrothumia,* which
expresses the steadfastness of the Christian in the midst of ill-
treatment. It is the divinely given ability of forbearance and
patient endurance when one is called upon to suffer wrongs.
Thayer says the word means the self-restraint which does not
hastily retaliate.[13] We should think of Jesus whose first word
from the cross was the prayer, "Father, forgive them; for they
know not what they do" (Luke 23: 34).

The Greek word *chrēstotēs,* gentleness, could be rendered
also benignity or kindness. It is from a verb meaning to use,
hence etymologically it has the idea of usableness, or kindness
in rendering service to others. It includes the thought of amia-
bility or pleasantness of disposition. Trench says it is a grace
which pervades the entire nature, mellowing there all that
would have been harsh and austere.[14] The adjective *chrēstos* is
used of wine which has been mellowed with age (Luke 5: 39),
and of Christ's yoke which is not harsh or irritating (Matt.
11: 30).

In rendering the Greek term *agathōsunē,* "goodness" seems
too general. Active benevolence seems to be the idea, as the
derivation from *agathos* (good) indicates the bestowal upon
others of that which is beneficial. Rendall takes it to mean
"goodness in the free bestowal of bounty on those who need."[15]
Barlow explains it as "the virtue whereby we communicate to
others good things, for their good and benefit.[16] Trench says a
person might manifest *agathōsunē,* zeal for goodness and truth,

---

[13]*Op. cit.,* p. 387.
[14]Richard Chenevix Trench, *Synonyms of the New Testament,* p. 233.
[15]Frederic Rendall, *The Expositor's Greek Testament,* Vol. III, p. 188.
[16]George Barlow, *The Preacher's Homiletic Commentary on Galatians,* p. 94.

in rebuking and correcting wrong; that Jesus was working in the spirit of this grace when he expelled the money-changers from the Temple court (Matt. 21:12-13) and when he uttered the invectives against the scribes and Pharisees (Chap. 23).[17]

For *pistis,* faith, in this context "faithfulness" is perhaps the better rendering. Some commentators think the term here means belief in the gospel, in contrast to the heresies of verse 20. Others think that it signifies trustworthiness, good faith in human relationships, due regard for the just claims of fellow men, faithfulness in carrying out promises, and the like. Williams, Goodspeed, and Revised Standard render it "faithfulness"; Weymouth, "good faith"; Moffatt and J. B. Phillips, "fidelity"; and A. S. Way, "trustfulness." *Pistis* means both "faith" and "faithfulness." Actually the one does not exist without the other. Faithfulness is faith in action.

The Greek word for meekness is *prautēs,* the quality of mild-, ness and reasonableness exhibited by a Christian. Meekness is the antithesis of self-reliance and arrogance. It denotes humility, receptivity, and submission to God's will and word. Trench says meekness is an inwrought grace of the soul, the exercises of which are first and chiefly towards God; that it is that temper of spirit in which we accept his dealings with us as good, and so without disputing or resisting.[18] Someone has defined meekness as "power under control." Of course the supreme example of meekness is Jesus himself. Barlow says, "Meekness is the other side of faith. It is not tameness and want of spirit; it comports with the highest courage and activity and is a qualification for public leadership."[19]

"Temperance" is better rendered "self-control," since the Greek *egkrateia* is a compound word meaning "holding in" or "maintaining control." Temperance is but one aspect of the self-mastery denoted by this term. The presence of the Holy Spirit enables the Christian to master all his desires and appetites. Such self-control "comprehends every form of temperance, and includes the mastery of all appetites, tempers, and passions."[20]

[17]*Op. cit.,* p. 234.
[18]Trench, *op. cit.,* p. 152.
[19]Barlow, *op. cit.,* p. 93.
[20]Rendall, *op. cit.,* p. 188.

CHAPTER V

Verbs

The chief part of a sentence is the verb, and all the rest of Greek syntax is built around it. Subject and predicate are the foci of the sentence, and each may be amplified by various other parts of speech.

The verb has two functions: It expresses action or state of being and makes affirmations. Action may be indicated also by substantives, adjectives, infinitives, and participles, but only the finite verb can express affirmation. "Verbs make affirmation by limiting the action to certain persons. This limitation is made by personal endings which also distinguish the voices."[1]

The Greek verb is an intricate piece of word mechanism. As an interpreter studies it analytically, he is thrilled at the many shades of meaning set forth by its various forms. Since it is the main word in a sentence, the verb is capable of more changes and hence of expressing a greater variety of meanings than the other words.

A Greek verb has mode, tense, and voice. Mode indicates the manner of affirmation—the manner in which an assertion is made—but does not necessarily involve the truth or falsity of the statement. Tense expresses the state of the action. Voice shows the relation of the action to the subject, whether the action is active, middle, or passive. The active voice represents the subject as acting. The middle voice represents the subject as acting with reference to himself. The passive voice represents the subject as acted upon.

It is essential that the student master the conjugation of the verb before he attempts exegesis, for without such a background exegesis is impossible. The study is enriched and actually becomes a delight when one bears in mind that he is

---

[1]RSG, p. 125.

dealing, not merely with Greek grammar and syntax, but with the words of divine revelation. Thus grammar becomes a thrilling means to a sublime purpose. With reasonable study one learns to find the verb stem around which the verb forms are built with architectural precision. Soon he becomes aware that by a series of suffixes and prefixes the various tenses, modes, voices, persons, and numbers are all clearly expressed.

Prepositions are often compounded with verbs. Such composition may emphasize the local force of the preposition; e.g., *ek* (out) plus *erchomai* (to go) becomes *exerchomai,* to go out. The composition may change the meaning of the verb and blend the preposition with it to give a resultant meaning. Sometimes the force of the preposition is weakened; e.g. *apo* (off, away from) combined with *dechomai* (to take, receive) means merely to take or accept, receive (*apodechomai*). Then there are prepositions in composition which are used in the perfective sense, intensifying and completing the idea expressed by the verb; e.g., *katergazesthe* in Philippians 2: 12, where the preposition *kata* with the verb *ergazomai* means "work out to completion," or "work on to the finish," [2] our salvation. There is the intensive force of *ek* in the charge made against Paul and Silas at Philippi, "These men, being Jews, do exceedingly trouble [*ektarassousin,* disturb, throw into confusion] our city" (Acts 16: 20).

The verb *strephō* (to turn, turn around), reflexively, turn oneself, i.e., change one's course of conduct, is common in the New Testament in composition with a number of prepositions (*ana, apo, dia, ek, epi, kata, meta, sun,* and *hupo*). *Epistrephō,* to turn, be converted, is common in the New Testament. The preposition *epi,* whose root meaning is "upon," used in the perfective sense with *strephō,* means "to turn thoroughly." In John 2: 15, the perfective use of the preposition *ana* (up, back, again) in composition with *strephō* intensifies the meaning of the verb and presents the picture of Jesus "upturning" the tables of the traffickers. Near the close of our Lord's earthly ministry he again cleansed the Temple court and overthrew (*katastrephō*—turned down) the tables of the money-changers (Matt. 21: 12). What a vivid picture of conversion this term

---

[2] RWP, Vol. IV, p. 446. Williams gives it, "Keep on working clear down to the finishing point of your salvation."

reveals. It is our word "catastrophe," thus showing the dynamic, revolutionary, thorough idea of conversion. Just as Jesus overthrew the devices of the money-changers and cleansed the Court of the Gentiles, so the human heart is changed in the catastrophic experience of conversion, and from man's inner nature are cast the evils of sin and Satan.

Another interesting compound is *katabrabeuetō*, rendered "beguile" in Colossians 2:18, its only appearance in the New Testament. *Brabeuō*, used only in Colossians 3:15, means "to be an umpire in a contest," and *kata* in composition in 2:18 has the idea of "down" (against). Thus, *katabrabeuetō* means to act as an umpire against one, or to frustrate a competitor for a prize in a contest. RWP[s] says, "Here it means to decide or give judgment against." In the light of the context, the thought seems to be: Do not allow heretical teachers to set forth the conditions on which the prize shall be yours. We might render the exhortation, Let no self-appointed umpire call you out! Moffatt says, "Let no one lay down rules for you as he pleases." Williams, "Stop letting anyone . . . defraud you as an umpire." Arthur S. Way, "Let no one cheat you of your heavenly prize." Revised Standard, "Let no one disqualify you."

In this connection, note Paul's use of the present imperative of *brabeuō* in Colossians 3:15, "Let the peace of Christ constantly act as umpire in your hearts." Thus the reliable arbiter is in the Christian's heart—it is the peace that the Christ gives. Goodspeed says, "Let the ruling principle in your hearts be Christ's peace." Weymouth, "Let the peace which Christ gives settle all questionings in your hearts." Moffatt, "Let the peace of Christ be supreme within your hearts."

In double compounds the meaning of a verb is amplified by the contribution of each additional preposition. For example, three times Paul uses the prepositions *sun* (together with) and *ana* (up) in composition with *mignumi* (to mix, mingle) in exhorting Christians not to associate with professing believers whose lives are beneath the standard of God's Word. The present middle infinitive, *sunanamignusthai*, with the negative is a strong indirect command. God's people are "not to be mixed up together with" people of questionable character (I Cor. 5:9, 11; II Thess. 3:14).

[s]Vol. IV, p. 496.

There is a vivid picture revealed in the use of *sun* (with) and *anti* (face to face, opposite from) in composition with the verb *lambanomai* in Luke 10:40. Martha requests the Lord to bid Mary "take hold at the other end [of the task, table] with me," an idea weakly rendered by the English "help." Paul uses this same double compound in Romans 8:26 where he says the Holy Spirit "takes hold at the other end [of the problem] with our weakness." What a marvelous revelation of the intercession of the Holy Spirit, and what a challenge to incite believers to pray! This same verb, *sunantilambanomai*, is used in Exodus 18:22 (LXX) where Jethro suggests that Moses provide assistants to "take hold with him" of the burdens involved in judging the multitudinous affairs of the Israelites.

A careful study of the distinction between verbs of similar meaning is rewarding. For example, *gameō* means "to marry," and *gamizō* means "to give in marriage." This distinction is observed in the New Testament (cf. Matt. 22:30; 24:38; Luke 17:27; 20:35), and must be kept in mind for a correct interpretation of I Corinthians 7:36-38. In the Corinthian passage it seems clear that Paul is giving advice to fathers or guardians of unmarried daughters. Revised Standard takes it as advice to a man and the girl to whom he is engaged. But such a position is precarious. It requires that *parthenos* (virgin) in verse 36 be rendered "betrothed" (RSV), and it carelessly renders *gamizō* in verse 38 "marry" as if the verb were *gameō*, although *gameō* has already been used five times in the chapter and is translated "marry" in verses 9, 28, and 36 (RSV) and again correctly in verse 39. Also the Revised Standard preserves the distinction between *gameō* and *gamizō* in Matthew 22:30; 24:38; Mark 12:25; Luke 17:27; 20:35.

The phrase "let them marry" (I Cor. 7:36) refers to the couple concerned in a given instance when a father gives his daughter in wedlock. That the passage considered refers to the duty of a father toward his daughter of marriageable age is the view of a number of authorities including Robertson, Farrar, Foster, and Lenski. New Testament translations setting forth this position include Williams, Weymouth, Montgomery, Confraternity, and Arthur S. Way.

Laleō and Legō

Though at times the verbs *laleō* and *legō* are used as synonyms, each has its distinctive connotation and much is gained when each is interpreted according to its specific meaning.

Laleō refers to the ability to employ the organs of speech, to give forth an utterance, emit a sound, or express words with the living voice.

Legō means to speak in the sense of declaring an intelligible message. While *laleō* emphasizes the outward form of speech, *legō* refers to the substance and meaning of that which is spoken. With *laleō* the fact of uttering articulate speech is the prominent notion, whereas with *legō* the main point is the correspondence of words to the thought of the speaker. *Laleō* refers to the act of speaking, while *legō* declares what the speaker actually says.

Thus *legō* means to speak articulately and intelligently, and although *laleō* is sometimes used in that way, *laleō* primarily refers to the articulation of sound. *Laleō* is ascribed not only to human language, but to the sounds made by animals, to the twittering and chirping of birds, to the humming or buzzing of insects, and to the noise made by inanimate objects like trees, pipes, flutes, and to an echo. *Laleō* is used of the sounding of a trumpet (Rev. 4:1), of the rumbling of thunder (10:3-4), of the beast which spoke like a dragon (13:11), and of the speech exercised by the beastly image (vs. 15). *Laleō* is an onomatopoetic word (formed in imitation of natural sounds, like our expressions "choo-choo" for train, "bow-wow" for dog), used by the Greeks of the jabbering of infants before they can speak distinctly. The root of the word is *lal,* illustrating the first efforts of a child to talk, as he says la, la, la.

The application of the distinction between *laleō* and *legō* helps clear up an otherwise difficult passage in First Corinthians. We still hear now and then the idea that women are forbidden by Paul to preach the gospel. Advocates of such a view quote I Corinthians 14:34-35 in defense of their position.

According to the general context of the New Testament, women are free to pray, witness, exhort, and preach, inasmuch as there is no distinction between men and women regarding salvation and the graces and gifts of the Holy Spirit (Gal.

3:28). Women are included in the commission of world evange-
lization (Acts 2:17-18). Philip the evangelist had four daughters who were preachers (21:9). To prophesy means to exhort,
witness, appeal, preach, according to I Corinthians 14:3. In
Romans 16:1-15 is a long list of gospel workers, men and
women, some of whom were probably preachers. In Philippians
4:3 Paul says, "Help those women which labored with me in
the gospel."

We are certain from Paul's letter itself that the Apostle approved of women preaching, for he implies that the women in
the church at Corinth took part in praying and preaching (I
Cor. 11:5). Exactly, therefore, what is Paul saying in I Corinthians 14:34-35? In the immediate context there are four keys
which unlock the passage: the meaning of the verb, the tense,
the situation which called forth the injunction, and the antithetical form of the prohibition.

First, note the verb used. Paul does not use *legō*, but *laleō*
which, as we have seen, means primarily to utter sounds, not
necessarily intelligible words. It is the onomatopoetic idea of
la-la-ing.

Second, Paul uses the present infinitive *lalein,* which tense
signifies continuous action. According to the force of this infinitive he says, "Let your women keep silence in the churches:
for it is not permitted to them to speak [to continue la-la-ing].
... It is a shame for women to speak [to go on la-la-ing] in the
church."

Third, note the situation which called forth the injunction.
Why such an exhortation? Because the women were disturbing
the church service by asking questions of their husbands during the preaching. In those days education, as always among
heathen peoples, was the privilege of the men. As an audience
listened with rapt attention to the wonderful gospel, the men
with their learning had little difficulty grasping the message.
Not so with the women. Hence their questions produced an
undertone of noise which was confusing to an audience. No
wonder Paul corrected them. So we see that the Apostle is not
dealing with the subject of women preaching, but with discipline. He is simply correcting disorder. He had already corrected the men in verses 32-33, "The spirits of the prophets are

subject to the prophets. For God is not the author of confusion, but of peace, as in all churches of the saints."

The fourth key is the antithetical form of the prohibition. An antithesis is a rhetorical device which presents two complementary statements, or as we might say, an antithesis has two equal arms. In the injunction of Paul here, one of these arms is prohibitory (vs. 34), and the other is permissive (vs. 35). The permission is: Ask their husbands at home. The prohibition is simply the converse: Don't ask them in church.

Agapaō and Phileō in John 21:15-17

There is an interesting use of the verbs *agapaō* and *phileō* in our Lord's reinstatement of Simon Peter as a preacher. Peter, after the crucifixion and resurrection of Jesus, had gone back to his nets (*halieuein,* the present infinitive of continuous action in John 21:3, might imply that Peter intended to remain with fishing as a vocation). He and his friends toiled all night and caught nothing. The appearance of Jesus on the lake shore next morning was a new summons to service in the gospel. Just as the Lord had previously given them a miraculous catch of fish at the initial call to discipleship (Luke 5:1-11), so now he repeats the miracle under similar circumstances and invites the apostolic band to a resumption of that fellowship which had been broken by his death.

Although the risen Lord had already appeared to Peter privately (Luke 24:34; I Cor. 15:5), on which occasion He doubtless restored him to personal fellowship, Jesus, now by the seaside, recommissions him in the presence of the other disciples.

Peter, always an impulsive and courageous individual, at the instant he realizes that his Lord is standing on the shore, abandons the net of fish for which he has been toiling and springs into the sea to greet Him. Such a hurried effort to get to the shore where the Master stood is a remarkable testimony to Peter's ardent affection, but Jesus wishes him to declare his devotion unmistakably.

After they had dined, our Lord, the master psychologist who knew how to bring out what was in man, began to probe Simon's deepest motive of discipleship. Jesus knew that only a complete surrender to himself would be adequate to carry

Simon and the other disciples through the temptations and crises of the future.

Jesus does not address Peter as Simon Petros (Simon the stone), but thrice addresses him as "Simon, son of John," his patronymic name. How this must have brought conviction to the heart of the big fisherman!

The question, "Lovest thou me more than these?" as far as the grammar reveals (*toutōn* being the form for both the masculine and neuter demonstrative pronouns), could mean, "Lovest thou me more than these other disciples love me?" or "Lovest thou me more than you love these things?" (i.e., this fishing boat, net, and temporal objects). Jesus asks, "Simon, son of John, do you love me with supreme and devoted love [*agapaō*]?" He is sounding the depths of Simon's heart to explode the last vestage of self-reliance (cf. Matt. 26:33) and to secure the humility so essential for Christian service. Peter replies, "Yes, Lord, thou knowest that I am fond of [*phileō*] thee." He does not repeat after Jesus the phrase "more than these"; neither does he use Jesus' strong word for love, but responds with the word which signifies love as friendship.

In his second question Jesus omits the "more than these" but again asks, "Lovest [*agapaō*] thou me?" Again Peter humbly replies, "Yes, Lord, thou knowest that I am fond of [*phileō*] thee." Jesus says, "Be a shepherd to my sheep." The command is in the present imperative, denoting durative action—Peter is to continue as a shepherd of Christ's sheep; this is to be his vocation.

In His third question Jesus takes Peter's word and asks, "Are you fond of [*phileō*] me? The interrogation implies, "Do you love me to the extent signified by *phileō*? Are you really sure that you are fond of me?" Peter is grieved deeply when he hears his own statement challenged, and doubtless recalls his three denials of discipleship on the morning of the crucifixion (Matt. 26:69 ff.). Now he repeats his allegiance to Jesus with the humble and sincere declaration, "Lord, thou knowest all things: thou knowest that I am fond of [*phileō*] thee." Jesus, with divine mercy and understanding, replies, "Feed my sheep."

Thus Peter was recommissioned as an apostle, and it was he whom God so mightily used to preach the powerful sermon on the Day of Pentecost when three thousand were saved. After being filled with the Holy Spirit, Simon indeed became the dependable disciple Jesus foresaw he would be when He gave him the name Peter (Aramaic, *Cephas;* Greek, *Petros*), meaning a stone.

It is the will of God that every Christian have this stable, rocklike character in order that it may be said also of us, "And yourselves, as living stones, are being built up a spiritual house, an holy priesthood, to offer up spiritual sacrifices acceptable to God by Jesus Christ" (I Pet. 2:5).

CHAPTER VI

Tense

One of the most significant features of the Greek language is tense. An understanding of this element of grammar will often solve what appears to be a serious problem of interpretation or enable the student to ascertain depths of meaning not possible otherwise.

No other language distinguishes the various relations of the verb so accurately as the Greek, for it is in the Greek that tense has had its most extensive development. It is exceedingly important that the interpreter grasp the precise function of each tense. He should proceed upon the principle that a New Testament writer, in a given instance, used a certain tense because it best expressed the idea he wished to convey.

The term "tense" (from the French *temps*, Latin *tempus*, time) is misleading, for time is not the fundamental idea. It is only in the indicative mode in Greek that the tenses denote time absolutely, and even in the indicative time is a secondary matter. The original and essential signification of the Greek tense is kind of action, or more specifically the state of the action, whether it is represented as a single act, as going on, or as finished. The verb root itself may express momentary, continuative, or completed action.

Originally there were two verb types, one denoting momentary or punctiliar action, and the other durative or linear action; just as in English "shut the door" depicts a different kind of action from "running a race." In Greek the kind of action expressed by the verb root or stem (*Aktionsart* as German grammarians have called it) involves the whole tense system (mode, participle, and infinitive).

Three essential kinds of action are expressed by the Greek tenses: (a) action contemplated in a single perspective, as a whole—point action (momentary or punctiliar); (b) action regarded as in progress, as a line (linear or durative); and (c) action represented as perfected (completed), which emphasizes its results or abiding state. Corresponding to these three viewpoints of action are the three basic tenses: aorist, present, and perfect. Punctiliar action is denoted by the aorist tense; durative action is denoted by the imperfect, present, and future tenses; and action in a state of completion is denoted by the perfect, pluperfect, and future perfect tenses.

Aorist Tense

According to its etymology, the term aorist (*aoristos,* without boundaries, unlimited) denotes simple, undefined action, with no consideration of its progress. The aorist represents action as a point (punctiliar), although it may have continued a long time. For example, a period of forty-six years is thus treated in John 2:20 where the aorist passive indicative refers to the construction of the Temple. And in Revelation 20:4 the period of a thousand years is viewed as a point, "they *lived* [aorist] and *reigned* [aorist] with Christ a thousand years." Many other illustrations show that the basic idea of the aorist is to denote an event as a whole, irrespective of the time involved in its accomplishment.

While the general function of the aorist is to express point action, there are distinctions of emphasis. Thus in a given context a verb in the aorist may emphasize the beginning of the action (inchoative or ingressive), the conclusion of the action (effective or culminative), or the action as a whole (constative). These three distinctions in punctiliar action are illustrated in the passage, "And the Word *became* flesh [ingressive aorist], and *dwelt* among us [constative aorist]. . . . And of his fullness have all we *received* [effective aorist]" (John 1:14, 16).

Often the ingressive aorist makes more forceful and meaningful the action of certain verbs. In John 11:35, well known as the shortest verse in the Bible, and a most significant one, the verb reveals a vivid picture of Jesus. The verb rendered "wept" is not *klaiō* (to weep audibly, mourn, lament, cry as a child), but it is the aorist of *dakruō* (to shed tears). With emphasis on the beginning of the action (ingressive aorist, *edakrusen*), it means that Jesus burst into tears. What a portrayal of the humanity of our Lord! He who is both God and man enters into the joys and sorrows of his disciples.

In II Corinthians 8: 9 we read that Jesus *became poor* (ingressive aorist). To say, "He was poor" would not only be an inadequate rendering; it would be untrue. But the ingressive emphasis is correct: He became poor. How rich he was! What an inexpressible condescension he made! And he did it willingly for us, through his love and grace, in order that we *might become rich* (ingressive aorist subjunctive).

In Romans 14: 9, *died* and *became alive* are aorists, denoting the momentary and once-for-all character of the atonement. The ingressive aorist indicative, *he became alive,* indicates that Jesus' conquest of death was complete. The ingressive aorist subjunctive, *"that he might become Lord* both of the dead and of the living," emphasizes the purpose of his glorious triumph.

The effective or culminative aorist, which places emphasis upon the end of an action, is illustrated in examples such as, *"I have gained"* (Matt. 25: 20); *"now they are hid"* (Luke 19: 42); *"having fulfilled* the ministration" (Acts 12: 25); *"they ceased* beating Paul" (21: 32); *"I learned* to be content" (Phil. 4: 11); "the Lion of the tribe of Judah . . . *has prevailed"* (Rev. 5: 5).

Many significant truths are brought out strikingly by the constative aorist. In Matthew 3: 17 the good pleasure of the Father regarding the Son and his incarnate ministry is expressed by the timeless force of *eudokēsa, "I was well pleased."* In John 3: 16 the aorist *edōken* (gave) is used because God's gift was a revealed fact. In that same verse "loved" (*ēgapēsen*) is constative aorist. It reaches back into the eternal past, extends across the scope of time including Bethlehem, Calvary, and the resurrection, and culminates in the eternal glory which awaits the people of God. How appropriately John 3: 16 has been called the gospel in a verse!

The aorist tense expresses not only punctiliar action, but is used to denote a sense of urgency. On the Day of Pentecost Peter, preaching to unregenerate people, says *Metanoēsate* ("Repent!"), using the aorist imperative, Do it now! (Acts 2: 38). There is a sense of urgency throughout the Lord's Prayer in which seven aorist imperatives are used (Matt. 6: 9-13).

The aorist is used to express maxims, aphorisms, or universal truths. We have such examples as, "If a man abide not in me, he is cast forth [aorist passive indicative] as a branch, and *is withered* [aorist passive indicative]" (John 15:6); and "The grass *withereth* [aorist passive indicative], and the flower thereof *falleth away* [aorist active indicative]" (I Pet. 1:24). Compare Luke 7:35, "But wisdom *is justified* [aorist indicative passive] of all her children." This idiom is called the gnomic aorist, gnomic being transliterated from the Greek term *gnōmē* which means a brief reflection, judgment, timeless truth.

In Romans 8:29-30 are five constative gnomic aorists: "foreknow . . . predestinate . . . called . . . justified . . . glorified." Paul sets forth God's work as complete from eternity. It embraces all believers, and involves the divine knowledge from before time to the consummation of the plan of salvation beyond time. Thus the glorification is expressed in the aorist although it is yet future from man's standpoint. This passage does not teach predestinarianism in the sense that human destiny is determined by a divine decree apart from the element of man's choice. It shows God's gracious purpose and the steps in its accomplishment. Paul considers it under five comprehensive acts, each of which rests logically upon the preceding one.

"Foreknow" (vs. 29) implies eternal advance knowledge (in harmony with omniscience), but it is certain that the term also means "to approve in advance." The verb *ginōskō*, to know, is used in the Scriptures in the sense of "approve" (cf. Ps. 1:6; Amos 3:2, LXX; Matt. 7:23; II Tim. 2:19). Hence the addition of the preposition *pro*, before, does not change the meaning of the verb, but places the act back in eternity. The entire expanse of time and the totality of temporal events were seen in the all-wise mind of God as finished and complete. Thus He beheld across the centuries those individuals who would serve him, and *approved in advance* (*proegnō*, timeless aorist) all those who would choose to be his servants. In regard to unbelievers, in eternity God knew about them in the sense of intellectual awareness (as would be signified by the verb *oida*, to know by intuition or reflection), but certainly did not foreapprove (*proegnō*) them.

The next aorist, *proōrisen* (Rom. 8:29), is the idea of "preplanned." Again it is the preposition *pro*, before, plus the verb *horizō*, to mark out boundaries or limits (our word horizon), hence *proōrisen* means "marked out in advance." God purposed from eternity that those whom he foreapproved should be conformed to the image of his Son. Moule says, "Let us banish from the idea of 'predestination' all thought of a mechanical pagan destiny, and use it of the sure purpose of the living and loving God."[1]

Another aorist, *ekalesen*, "called" (vs. 30), emphasizes the third step in the accomplishment of God's plan. In Pauline theology "calling" means more than "invitation"; it includes the acceptance of the divine call: "effectually drew so as truly and freely to choose Christ" (Moule).[2]

The fourth gnomic aorist here is "justified"—declared righteous. Lenski quotes the following definition: " 'Justification is that act of God by which he, of pure grace, for the sake of the merits of Christ, pronounces a poor sinner, who truly believes in Christ, free from guilt and declares him just.' "[3]

The final gnomic aorist of the series is "glorified." This refers to the crowning act of redemption. The time element is no problem in the light of the timeless aorist. Although glorification is yet future, it is expressed in the aorist because in the divine mind the plan of salvation is seen as complete from eternity. There is no afterthought with God. He sees the saved—all of them—from the beginning until the end of time. "We see through His sight, in hearing His word about it."[4]

Imperfect Tense

The imperfect indicative denotes incompleted action. Compared with the aorist indicative which expresses punctiliar action in past time, the imperfect portrays durative action in past time. In other words, the imperfect is the descriptive tense in historical narrative. The time element is prominent in the imperfect inasmuch as it is used only in the indicative mode.

Robertson says, "The aorist tells the simple story. The imperfect draws the picture. It helps you to see the course of the act. It passes before the eye the flowing stream of history."[5] "In juxtaposition the aorist lifts the curtain and the imperfect

[1] Handley C. G. Moule, *The Epistle to the Romans*, p. 238.
[2] *Loc. cit.*
[3] R. C. H. Lenski, *The Interpretation of St. Paul's Epistle to the Romans*, p. 563.
[4] H. C. G. Moule, *op. cit.*, p. 239.
[5] R, p. 883.

continues the play."[6] For example, there is "slumbered and
slept" (ingressive aorist, *began to nod,* and the imperfect, *continued sleeping*) (Matt. 25:5).

The force of the imperfects sketches vividly the scene of
John's ministry at the Jordan River: "John *had* [*eichen*, as was
his custom] his raiment of camel's hair. . . . Then *went out*
[*exeporeueto*] Jerusalem, and all Judea, and all the region
round about Jordan, and *were baptized* [*ebaptizonto*] of him
in Jordan" (Matt. 3:4-6). The linear force of the imperfect
tense pictures the streams of people who were going out to
John's baptism.

In Luke 17:27, four imperfects impressively reveal the life
of Noah's day: *They were eating (ēsthion), they were drinking (epinon), they were marrying (egamoun), they were giving
in marriage (egamizonto)*. The other verbs in the verse are
aorists: *entered, came, destroyed.* In verses 28-29 there is the
same contrast between the imperfects, *eating, drinking, buying,
selling, planting, building,* and the aroists, *went out, rained,
destroyed.*

The imperfect tense shows the important part Joseph played
in the Savior's birth. Joseph, noble man that he was, took the
virgin as his betrothed and protected her during the period in
which she needed understanding. He "did as the angel of the
Lord had bidden him, and took unto him his wife: and *knew
her not* [*know* is a euphemistic expression for the normal
intimacy of marriage] till she had brought forth her first-born
son: and he called his name Jesus" (Matt. 1:24-25). The imperfect of linear action (*ouk eginōsken autēn, he did not know
her*) shows that Joseph lived in continence with the virgin
until after the birth of the Savior.

The inchoative imperfect accents the commencement of an
action, e.g., Mark 14:35, where Jesus is described as falling
(*epipten,* vivid picture) upon the ground, and beginning to
pray (*proseucheto*) or continuing in prayer.

The conative imperfect is used of attempted action, or of
action begun but interrupted, e.g., "And they *gave* [*edidoun,*
were offering] him to drink wine mingled with myrrh: but he
received it not" (Mark 15:23); "They *sought* [*ezētoun*] again
to take him: but he escaped out of their hand" (John 10:39).

---

[6]R, p. 838.

Paul "reasoned in the synagogue every sabbath, and *persuaded* [*epeithen*, he was trying to persuade] the Jews and the Greeks" (Acts 18:4).

Another interesting idiom is the potential imperfect, illustrated in Paul's statement in Romans 9:3, "I *could wish* [*ēuchomēn*, I was on the point of wishing] that myself were accursed from Christ for my brethren, my kinsmen according to the flesh." "He holds himself back from the abyss by the tense."[7]

The periphrastic form[8] of the imperfect makes more emphatic the durative idea of the tense. Thus there is stressing of continuous action by the use of *ēn* (third person singular imperfect of the verb "to be") with the present participle in expressions like *"he was teaching"* (Matt. 7:29); *"he had* many possessions" (19:22); "heart *was constantly burning"* (Luke 24:32).

Present Tense

The present is the normal tense for incompleted or linear action in all the modes. But a further word must be said. While the basic idea of the present tense is that of progress, such is not its only signification. Inasmuch as the indicative mode has no distinctive tense for point action in present time, the present tense is used to perform that function. However, the progressive force of the present tense is primary, especially in the potential modes. "In them the aorist serves the purpose for the punctiliar tense under all circumstances, since they have no temporal significance."[9] So it can be remembered that in the subjunctive, imperative, and optative modes, and in participles and infinitives, the aorist is punctiliar, and the present is almost always linear.

The descriptive force of the present tense is seen frequently. *"We are perishing"* (Matt. 8:25) shows the disciples' realization of approaching doom as the waves are engulfing them. "Our lamps *are going out"* (25:8) pictures "the sputtering, flickering, smoking wicks"[10] and emphasizes the tragedy of spiritual unpreparedness. Paul's use of the present tense indicates his

---

[7]R, p. 886.
[8]Periphrasis (from *peri*, around, plus *phrazō*, to declare, is the use of a longer phrasing in place of a possible shorter one; a round-about expression, circumlocution, redundancy.
[9]D-M, p. 181.
[10]RWP, Vol. I, p. 197.

concern at the decadence of the Galatians. He says, *"I am marveling* [it is a constant amazement to me] that you are so quickly in the process of removing yourselves[11] from him who called you by the grace of Christ, unto another gospel (Gal. 1:6). The tense implies that the retrogression, although in progress, is not yet completed. Paul endeavors to save the situation in Galatia before it becomes hopeless.

Among special uses of the present tense is the historical present. This idiom relates a past event in the present tense for vividness: "In those days *comes along* [*paraginetai*] John the Baptizer, *preaching* [*kērussōn*, present participle] in the wilderness of Judea" (Matt. 3:1). The writer of the Fourth Gospel is fond of the dramatic historical present, e.g., the verbs *sees . . . coming . . . says* (John 1:29); the portrayal of Jesus as he is *passing along* (9:1). With a series of presents John describes the excitement of the disciples at the empty tomb: Mary Magdalene *comes . . . she sees* the stone has been taken away *. . . she runs . . .* and *she says* (20:1-2); John *sees* the linen garments lying . . . Simon Peter *comes . . .* and *beholds* (keeps looking at) the linen bands (vss. 5-6). The presence and undisturbed condition of the burial garments were evidences of the resurrection. Indeed, Jesus was risen from the dead! In Romans 7:14-23, the Apostle Paul uses the historical present tense in his vivid description of the spiritual battle which once raged in his life.

The present tense is used to express timeless being. Jesus says, "Before Abraham *came to be* [*genesthai*, aorist infinitive], *I am*" (*egō eimi*, present tense, and double nominative for emphasis). The aorist indicates a beginning for the existence of Abraham, but the present tense emphasizes the eternal pre-existence of Jesus.

The gnomic present is used to express timeless truths; e.g., "Every good tree *bringeth forth* good fruit; but a corrupt tree *bringeth forth* evil fruit" (Matt. 7:17); "God *loves* a cheerful giver" (II Cor. 9:7). The Greek word rendered "cheerful" is *hilaros*, our word "hilarious" being a transliteration of this graphic term.

---

[11]Middle voice. If it is taken as passive voice, the translation would be *being removed.*

The prophetic present adds force to a statement or promise. To those who go forth to do his will Jesus says, "Behold, I am [*egō eimi*] with you all the days until the consummation of the age" (Matt. 28:20). What a blessed and comforting promise! The very Christ whom the disciples were beholding in his glorified person and who holds all authority in heaven and earth, promises to be at their side and with the church throughout the gospel age. The position of *egō*, I, in the sentence makes it decidedly positive, and the use of the double nominative (I myself) adds still more to the emphasis. Robertson's comments on the Savior's promise are pointed and appropriate:

> He is to be with the disciples when he is gone, with all the disciples, with all knowledge, with all power, with them all the days (all sorts of days, weakness, sorrows, joy, power), till the consummation of the age. . . . This blessed hope is not designed as a sedative to an inactive mind and complacent conscience, but an incentive to the fullest endeavor to press on to the farthest limits of the world that all the nations may know Christ and the power of his Risen Life.[12]

Perfect Tense

The perfect tense conveys the idea of completed action with abiding results. "The action may have been completed a moment ago or a thousand years ago." It may be represented as just finished or as standing finished, and the resultant idea may be state or condition.[13]

It is important to remember that the perfect tense denotes an action as completed at the time of the speaker or writer. Dana and Mantey say, "Its basal significance is the progress of an act or state to a point of culmination and the existence of its finished results. That is, it views action as a finished product.[14]

Let us notice a few illustrations of the force of this interesting tense. John the Baptizer says, *Tetheamai,* "I beheld, and the vision remains with me, the Spirit descending as a dove out of heaven" (John 1:32). He emphasizes again the continuing character of spiritual experience when he says, *Heōraka,* "I saw, and it is as though I were still beholding it," and *memartureka,* "I gave witness and continue to do so that He is the Son of God" (vs. 34).

---

[12]RWP, Vol. I, p. 246.
[13]RSG, p. 143.
[14]D-M, p. 200.

Jesus overcomes the tempter by quoting the Word of God. Our Lord's significant expression *gegraptai* (Matt. 4: 4, 7, 10) means, "It was written and remains thus!" God's Word stands written. It has been recorded and the record abides. The expression "refers to the results of a process of divine inspiration whereby the Old Testament Scriptures are in existence."[15] Likewise we have the New Testament by divine inspiration.

In Pilate's well-known expression, "What I have written I have written" (John 19: 22), the two perfects accent the decisiveness and unalterableness of the Roman governor's action.

Jesus' sixth word from the cross is uttered in the perfect tense. *Tetelestai* (John 19: 30) means, "It is finished and remains finished!" The purpose of God in the cross is completed, consummated, and perfected forever; and the infinite results continue through all time and eternity, effectual for all who are trusting in the merits of Jesus' sacrifice.

In I Corinthians 15: 3-4, Paul's change of tense is significant. He says that Christ *died* (aorist, accenting the once-for-allness of his death); that *he was buried* (aorist, the fact of the entombment); and that *he has been raised* (perfect tense) *and still lives*, thus emphasizing the permanence of the resurrection and its consequences. It is because Christ died as a sacrifice for our sins that his resurrection accomplishes our salvation.

Also note John's *akēkoamen, heard and it is still ringing in our ears; heōrakamen, seen and the vision remains before us* (I John 1: 1-3); and *ēi peplērōmenē*, perfect passive subjunctive, "that your [best text has 'our'] joy *may be full*" (*made complete and remain in that state*) (vs. 4. Same verb form is used in John 16: 24, where it refers clearly to *your* joy).

In speaking of the accomplishments of Christ through his ministry Paul says, "So that from Jerusalem and in a circle as far as Illyricum, *I have fulfilled with abiding results* [*peplērōkenai*, perfect active infinitive] (my commission in) the gospel of Christ" (Rom. 15: 19). Among Paul's last words, as he nears the sunset of his brilliant career, are four verbs in the perfect tense: "The time of my departure *is at hand* [has come, is already present]. *I have fought . . . I have finished . . . I have kept*" (II Tim. 4: 6-7). These expressions,

---

[15]D-M, p. 191.

written from the prison cell and in the realization of approaching martyrdom, have inspired and challenged all succeeding generations. Think of what was accomplished through the life of Paul! The results cannot be estimated adequately. The world needs ministers today who can preach and build New Testament congregations with permanent results.

Future Tense

As the name implies, the future tense is used to affirm that an action is going to take place. Because the future is primarily an indicative tense, and because of the very nature of the tense as a statement which generally denotes what is going to happen, the element of time is prominent.

In some verbs the future tense is formed on punctiliar roots, and in other verbs it is formed on durative roots. Thus while the kind of action denoted by the future may be either punctiliar or durative, it is usually punctiliar. Robertson says the future tense is "fundamentally punctiliar in idea." [16] According to Burton, any instance of the future which is not clearly progressive should be accounted as aoristic. [17]

Several shades of meaning are expressed by the future tense. It may be simply futuristic (statement that an event will transpire in the future); it may be volitive (when it gives a command, as in Matt. 5: 43; Jas. 2: 8); or it may be deliberative (when used to ask a question, rhetorical or otherwise. Cf. John 6: 68; Rom. 6: 2). Also the future may be used in the gnomic sense, to express a timeless truth, or what will happen under certain conditions (e.g., Rom. 5: 7; 7: 3; Gal. 6: 5).

Pluperfect Tense

The pluperfect (or past perfect) tense represents an action completed and the results of the action in existence up to a prescribed point in the past. Inasmuch as the pluperfect never occurs except in the indicative mode, it always has time significance.

The pluperfect was not widely used in Koine Greek, but it is a very interesting tense. It fills in certain elements of the

---

[16]R, p. 353.
[17]Ernest DeWitt Burton, *Syntax of the Moods and Tenses in New Testament Greek*, p. 32.

background or setting of an action, supplying additional information for a reader. As Robertson says, it takes the reader " 'behind the scenes' " as it is often thrown in parenthetically.[18] Notice the pluperfects: "His disciples *had gone away*" (John 4:8); *"it had become* dark already, and Jesus *had not come* to the disciples" (6:17). Judas' prearranged agreement to betray Jesus is shown by *dedōkei,* "he had given them a token" (Mark 14:44). The disciples' awareness of Saul's intent is reflected in *elēluthei, had come* (Acts 9:21). This same form is used in 8:27 with the future participle, expressing the purpose for which the Ethiopian had come to Jerusalem. Note also *pepisteukeisan, they had believed* (14:23), indicating that the elders had already put their trust in the Lord before they were formally and publicly set apart for the ministry. And so it is believed today that the ceremony of ordination is human recognition of a divine call.

Tenses Illumine Doctrine of Salvation

Let us notice several additional examples of the significance of tense in its doctrinal or theological implications. The force of the aorist and of the present tense is clear in Romans 3:23, "For all *have sinned* [*hēmarton,* constative aorist as in 5:12], and *come short* [*husterountai,* present indicative, continue to fall short] of the *glory* [*doxēs,* standard] of God." This statement summarizes the experience of the whole race in one timeless aorist, and by use of the present tense shows that mankind still falls short of the divine standard.

In Romans 6:15, the deliberative subjunctive is aorist, *hamartēsōmen,* and prohibits even an act of sin. We might translate this verse, "In the light of this fact, what is to be our course of action? Shall we commit occasional acts of sin because we are not under legal principle but under God's favor? Never!"

Notice again the divine standard in I John 2:1: "My little children, these things I write unto you in order that you *sin not at all* [*mē hamartēte,* aorist subjunctive, not even one act of sin]. However, if any man *commits an act of sin* [aorist subjunctive], we have an Advocate with the Father, Jesus Christ the righteous."

---

[18]R, p. 905.

Jesus emphasizes two aspects of discipleship by the tenses he uses: "If any man will come after me, *let him deny* [aorist imperative, deny once and for all] himself, and *take up* [aorist imperative, one all-inclusive act] his cross, and follow [present imperative, keep on following] me" (Matt. 16:24). Luke 9:23 adds the expression "daily" to the exhortation to take up the cross. Thus we see that discipleship involves two basic ideas: (1) A definite, once-for-all decision at a point in time, and (2) constant, continuing, day-by-day commitment. Thus is taught both the crisis experience of discipleship and the abiding attitude of surrender which characterizes the entire lifetime of the believer.

An awareness of the tense used is essential for an interpretation of I John 3:6, 9. John says, "Everyone who *continues abiding* [*menōn*, present participle] in him does not *go on sinning* [*hamartanei*, durative present]; everyone who *goes on sinning* [*hamartanōn*, present participle] is not *in the state of having seen* [*heōraken*, perfect tense] *him*, nor *in the state of having known* [*egnōken*, perfect again] him (vs. 6)." In verse 9 the Apostle says, "Everyone who *is in the state of having been begotten* [*gegennēmenos*, perfect passive participle] of God does not *practice* [*poiei*, present of linear action] *sin*, because his seed remains in him; and he is not able *to go on sinning* [*hamartanein*, present infinitive] because he *is in the state of having been begotten* [*gegennētai*, perfect passive indicative] of God."

Saving faith involves both the initial act of believing in (receiving) the Lord Jesus Christ and the continuous attitude of trusting in him. In Romans 10:9-10, Paul says, *"If thou shalt confess* [aorist subjunctive] with thy mouth the Lord Jesus, and *shalt believe* [aorist subjunctive] in thine heart that God hath raised him from the dead, *thou shalt be saved* [future passive indicative, which expresses actuality]. For with the heart man *believeth* [present indicative passive and impersonal construction, *faith goes on being exercised*] unto righteousness; and with the mouth *confession is made* [again present indicative passive, and impersonal construction, *confession keeps being made*] unto salvation." Justification is by faith alone, and the believer is justified the moment he exercises faith. But the term salvation (*sōtēria*) in the New

Testament indicates not only present or initial salvation, but ultimate salvation (Matt. 10: 22; 24: 13; Mark 13: 13; Rom. 13: 11; Heb. 9: 28; I Pet. 1: 5, 9, 10). In other words, the believer remains in the state of justification as long as he is faithful to his Lord.

In John 3: 15 the tense implication is clear as Jesus says that everyone *who goes on believing* (*pisteuon,* present participle) *may keep on having* (*echēi,* present subjunctive) eternal life. The New Testament connotation of eternal life is not primarily that of endless existence. The expression refers basically to the quality of life. In John 17: 3, Jesus says, "And this is life eternal, that they *might know* [present active subjunctive, *should continue knowing* in intimate personal experience, *ginōskō*] thee the only true God, and Jesus Christ, whom thou hast sent."

There is no contradiction between Paul and James regarding salvation by faith (cf. Rom. 4: 1 ff. and Jas. 2: 21 ff.). They take different incidents in the life of Abraham and set forth complementary views of the same problem. Paul is thinking of faith as a basis for salvation, a placing of faith, faith in its logical form; James is thinking of faith as evidence of salvation, a vindication of faith, faith in its practical form. It is well to remember that faith is both a medium (the means of entrance into grace) and a channel (the means of continuous blessings in grace).

"Cease Clinging to Me"

An understanding of the significance of tense clears away a contradiction which some translations (e.g., King James, English Revised, American Standard, Confraternity) make between John 20: 17 and Matt. 28: 9. Jesus' words to Mary Magdalene, *Mē mou haptou* (John 20: 17) do not contradict Matthew's account which says the Marys held Jesus by the feet and worshiped him. The verb *haptō* means not only "to touch," but "to cling to." In John the latter idea is evidently meant as indicated by the present tense. *Mē* is a prohibitive or negative particle. *Haptou* is the present imperative which denotes linear action. Bearing each of these elements of syntax in mind, the total idea expressed in Jesus' exhortation is, "Stop holding to me," or "Cease clinging to me." From the composite picture revealed by the parallel accounts we see what happened: On the morning of the resurrection Jesus appeared to the Marys and they grasped his feet and worshiped him. After accepting their adoration, Jesus says to Mary, "Cease clinging to me; for I have not yet *ascended to my Father to stay* [force of *anabebēka*, perfect tense]; but go to my brethren and say to them, I ascend to my Father and your Father, and to my God and your God." Jesus wanted the other disciples to hear the good news of the resurrection.

Disruption of Marriage

Greek tense and voice shed light on the problem of marriage disruption for an innocent person. In I Corinthians 7:15 Paul says, "If the unbeliever *separates himself* [*chōrizetai*, present middle indicative], *let the separation take its course* [*chōrizesthō*, present middle imperative]; the brother or the sister *does not remain in bondage* [*ou dedoulōtai*, perfect passive indicative] in such circumstances." In addition to the force of the perfect tense, *dedoulōtai* is placed at the beginning of the Apostle's sentence for strong emphasis. Willful disruption of the marriage union by the unbeliever sets the other spouse free. From this many would infer that the Christian spouse, thus released, may marry again.

Paul adds, "But God has called us in peace." The perfect tense of *called* (*keklēken*) reflects the superlative will of God, "permanent call in the sphere or atmosphere of peace."[19] A disrupted marriage is a sin against the persons involved, a sin against society, and a sin against the will and Word of God. The divine plan of marriage intends that the union should be permanent. Certainly a Christian spouse, motivated by kindness and consideration, will do everything legitimately possible to prevent a breakup of marriage. But if all efforts fail, the believer is free.

Binding and Loosing

Misunderstanding in much of Christendom has long been associated with Jesus' words about binding and loosing in Matthew 16:19 and 18:18. The participles in those passages have been traditionally rendered as though they were simple futures, viz., "shall be bound . . . shall be loosed" (King James, English Revised, American Standard, Revised Standard, Confraternity; same idea in Weymouth, Moffatt, Montgomery, Goodspeed, and others).

But these participles are not simple future verbs. They are future perfect passive participles, and in light of this, the translation of Matthew 16:19 would go like this: "I will give you [singular] the keys of the kingdom of heaven, but[20] whatever *you may bind* [*dēsēis,* aorist active subjunctive] on earth *shall have been bound* [*estai dedemenon,* periphrastic future perfect passive] in heaven, and whatever *you may loose* [*lusēis,* aorist active subjunctive] on earth *shall have been loosed* [*estai lelumenon,* periphrastic future perfect passive] in heaven."

Likewise the translation of Matthew 18:18 is: "Verily I say to you [plural personal pronoun], whatsoever *you may bind* [*dēsēte,* aorist active subjunctive] upon earth *shall have been bound* [*estai dedemena,* periphrastic future perfect passive] in heaven, and whatsoever *you may loose* [*lusēte,* aorist active subjunctive] upon earth *shall have been loosed* [*estai lelumena,* periphrastic future perfect passive] in heaven."

Thus Matthew 16:19 and 18:18 are seen to be in harmony with the general tenor of the New Testament which nowhere teaches sacerdotalism. "Binding" and "loosing" are used metaphorically of course, in the passages, meaning "prohibiting" and "permitting." All that is proclaimed by the ministry and church must be based on the Lord's authority.

Professor Mantey has pointed out that Matthew 16:19 and 18:18 were rendered incorrectly in the Latin Vulgate Version by Jerome about A.D. 400. Concerning that regrettable error, Dr. Mantey adds: "No doubt millions of people have been misled by believing their sins were forgiven by God, when some religious leader had pronounced their sins forgiven, in spite of the fact that they had not met the conditions of God's forgiveness."[21]

There are serious theological implications in the traditional

---

[20]Rendering the conjunction *kai* adversatively, which best fits the context. Such is a frequent use of *kai* in Koine Greek.
[21]WPAP, p. 51.

rendering. Has any religious communion or its clergy been authorized by the Lord Jesus Christ to remit or to retain men's sins? Has any ecclesiastical body the prerogative to impart salvation in God's behalf? Can any institution or its representatives make pronouncements which heaven is bound to ratify? If the common rendering of the passages in question is true, disciples on earth are given authority over heaven! But is not the converse true? Does not the general tenor of the New Testament indicate that heaven is our authority and that God determines the policy of the ministry and church? According to the Scriptures, it is the function of the clergy to set forth the terms of salvation, making known what God has declared. Man is only the servant or ambassador of the Almighty. God is sovereign, and gives to no human being the prerogative of pronouncing the salvation or the damnation of any soul. Clergymen, therefore, are not judges who decide the destinies of their hearers. They are proclaimers of salvation on divine terms.

The two verses under consideration, as traditionally rendered and interpreted, are strongholds for advocates of sacerdotalism. What are the implications of the Greek tenses in these passages?

The phrases commonly rendered "shall be bound . . . shall be loosed" are not simple future tenses, but are periphrastic future perfect passive participles. They should be translated as such, and the interpreter should bring forth the total idea conveyed by such a construction. The same participles and constructions are found in both passages, the only difference being that in Matthew 16:19 the participles are singular because Peter is addressed, while in 18:18 the participles are plural because the group of disciples is addressed.

It is precarious to treat these participles as though they were simple futures and give them a figurative or irregular rendering. There should be no interpretative problem regarding the tense of the participles. If the Greek writer wished to convey the thought expressed by the simple future, why did he not use that tense? Had he desired to express the idea conveyed by the present or simple future, those forms were at his disposal. We must assume that because of the significance of the perfect, that was the tense the Greek writer wished to use to express precisely what he had in mind.

Dana and Mantey have pointed out that "perhaps nothing has been better preserved in Greek than the idiomatic force of the tenses. . . . A sufficiently close examination, with the genius of the tense in mind, will generally reveal a significant reason for each variation." [22]

It is difficult to understand why so many translators have failed to render the passages adequately. We can only conclude that the common view became so entrenched in tradition that many scholars overlooked the force of the Greek perfect tense. No wonder Dana and Mantey say, "The judgment of tense is one of the realms in which the gravest errors have occurred in the translation and interpretation of the New Testament," and "Winer is unquestionably just in bringing charge that at this point 'New Testament grammarians and expositors have been guilty of the greatest mistakes.' " [23] Robertson says, "Probably nothing connected with syntax is so imperfectly understood by the average student as tense." [24]

However, it is significant that although many commentators have accepted the traditional rendering of Matthew 16: 19 and 18: 18, "nevertheless the majority of them in their comments declared that we cannot assume that men's decisions are final, but rather that it is imperative that they coincide with the divine will." [25] A. B. Bruce holds that judgments to be valid in heaven must be "in accordance with the truth of things." [26]

We have already pointed out that the perfect tense conveys the idea of completed action with abiding results, and that the point of completion is always antecedent to the time of the speaker or writer. It is important to remember that the perfect denotes what began in the past and still continues. As Gildersleeve put it, " 'The perfect looks at both ends of an action.' " Robertson quotes Blass as saying it " 'unites in itself as it were present and aorist, since it expresses the continuance of completed action.' " [27]

In some contexts the action of the perfect refers clearly to something done in the past. . . . In other contexts the action of the perfect refers to the abiding results of something that happened in the past. . . . But the

[22]D-M, p. 208.
[23]D-M, p. 207.
[24]R, p. 821.
[25]WPAP, p. 47.
[26]EGT, Vol. I, p. 225.
[27]R, p. 893.

perfect, regardless of which phase is dominant, is never only one or the other. It always implies both past action and abiding results, although one or the other may stand out according to the setting. The notion of continuance arises from the simple force of the perfect, but a completed action is a vital part of the warp and woof, the very genius of the perfect itself and the foundation of a permanent state. . . . It . . . has its roots in the past and implies past action.[28]

Whereas the perfect tense contemplates an action that is complete at the time of the speaker, the future perfect simply projects the whole unit into the future and conceives an act which will have been completed at the time contemplated in the future and of which the results will abide.[29]

It is encouraging to know that an increasing number of scholars have realized the implications of the Greek perfect tense for New Testament interpretation, as the following evidence shows:

"J. B. Rotherham (1893): 'And whatsoever thou mayest bind upon the earth shall have been bound in the heavens, and whatsoever thou mayest loose upon the earth shall have been loosed in the heavens.' (*The New Testament Critically Emphasized*)."[30]

"A. S. Worrell (1904): 'And whatsoever you shall bind on the earth shall have been bound in heaven, and whatsoever you shall loose on the earth shall have been loosed in heaven.' (*Worrell's Translation of the New Testament*)."[31]

In 1922 an article by J. R. Mantey, "The Perfect Tense Ignored in Matthew 16: 19; 18: 18 and John 20: 23," was published in *The Expositor* (London), Vol. XXIII. In December 1938 in Union Theological Seminary, New York City, at a joint session of the Society of Biblical Literature and Exegesis and the Linguistic Society of America, Professor Mantey presented a paper, "The Mistranslation of the Perfect Tense in John 20: 23; Matthew 16: 19 and 18: 18." A few months later, in 1939, his presentation was published in the *Journal of Biblical Literature,* Vol. LVIII.

C. H. Cadoux, in his book, *Catholicism and Christianity,* (1929, page 386), has this significant observation quoted by Dr. Mantey:

Taken by themselves, therefore, the words of Matthew 18: 18 mean that the community will in the solution of its ethical problems, come only to

[28]WPAP, p. 41.
[29]Wilber T. Dayton, *The Asbury Seminarian,* Vol. II, No. 2, (1947), p. 87.
[30]WPAP, p. 51.
[31]*Loc. cit.*

such decisions as have already been sanctioned and approved by God. That is the meaning required, strictly speaking, by the future perfect tenses used: it is somewhat doubtful whether we are entitled to treat them—as writers usually do—as if they were simple futures, for in that case why did not the author take the simple futures, *dethēsetai* (shall be bound) and *luthēsetai* (shall be loosed)? Only if we are warranted in ignoring the distinction of tenses, can we interpret the words as meaning that whatever the community (or Peter) decides, God will subsequently, as it were, endorse.[32]

B. W. Bacon of Yale, in his *Studies in Matthew* (1930, page 302), reflected the force of the perfect tense in his rendering of the principal clauses of 16:19: " 'Whatever thou dost prohibit on earth will have been prohibited in heaven, and whatever thou dost permit on earth will have been permitted in heaven.' "[33]

Charles B. Williams, *The New Testament: A Translation in the Language of the People* (1937),[34] gives clear renderings: "Whatever you forbid on earth must be what is already forbidden in heaven, and whatever you permit on earth must be what is already permitted in heaven." (16:19) "Whatever you forbid on earth must be already forbidden in heaven, and whatever you permit on earth must be already permitted in heaven" (18:18).

Professor Chamberlain comments on the periphrastic future perfect construction of 16:19 in the following words:

This is wrongly translated "shall be bound" and "shall be loosed," seeming to make Jesus teach that the apostles' acts will determine the policies of heaven. They should be translated "shall have been bound" and "shall have been loosed." This makes the apostles' acts a matter of inspiration or heavenly guidance. Cf. Matthew 18:18. This incorrect translation has given expositors and theologians a great deal of trouble.[35]

Doctor Wuest brings out the force of the perfect tenses in Matthew 16:19 and 18:18:

Whatever you bind on earth [forbid to be done], shall have been already bound [forbidden to be done] in heaven; and whatever you loose on earth [permit to be done], shall have already been loosed in heaven [permitted to be done].

Whatever you forbid on earth, shall have already been forbidden in

---

[32]WPAP, p. 51f.
[33]*Ibid.*, p. 52.
[34]Copyright assigned, 1949, to Moody Bible Institute, Chicago, Illinois.
[35]William Douglas Chamberlain, *An Exegetical Grammar of the Greek New Testament*, p. 80.

heaven. And whatever you permit on earth, shall have already been permitted in heaven.[36]

In 1945, Wilber T. Dayton, a doctoral candidate at Northern Baptist Theological Seminary, Chicago, Illinois, completed his dissertation entitled, "The Greek Perfect Tense in Relation to John 20:23, Matthew 16:19 and 18:18." Mr. Dayton also summarized his work in an article under the title of "John 20:23; Matthew 16:19 and 18:18 in the Light of the Greek Perfect Tenses."[37] His research, which he says "is naturally a sequel to and extension of Mantey's articles," has made a significant contribution to the field of New Testament interpretation. Mr. Dayton not only consulted all the Greek grammars at his disposal, but made a thorough, inductive study of the perfect tense in Koine Greek literature, including selections from Strabo, Philo, Josephus, the Septuagint, Apostolic Fathers, papyri, and Apocrypha. He makes this summary statement: "Neither from the Greek grammars, nor the classical illustrations, nor the Koine studies has any reason been found to deny Mantey's statement that 'the perfect tense pictures a past action, the result of which was present to the speaker or writer.'" Regarding the interpretation of Matthew 16:19 and 18:18, Dr. Dayton says in the same article:

> They [the apostles] were not to exceed their authority but were to forbid what God would have already forbidden and permit what God would have already permitted. They were to be heralds, preachers, ambassadors—not priests with authority to bind God by their acts of priestly absolution.

Perfect Tense in John 20:23

The verbs *apheōntai* and *kekratēntai* in the principal clauses of John 20:23 have been commonly rendered as if they were present tense, viz., "they are remitted . . . they are retained." But the verbs are perfects[38] and a proper translation will reflect the force of the tense as follows: *"Anyone's* sins *you* [plural] *may forgive* [*aphēte,* aorist subjunctive], *they have been forgiven* [*apheōntai,* perfect passive indicative] to them; *any-*

---

[36]Kenneth S. Wuest, *The Gospels: An Expanded Translation,* pp. 81, 85. The brackets are Wuest's.

[37]*The Asbury Seminarian,* Vol. II, No. 2, pp. 74-89.

[38]There are some manuscripts which give *aphientai* (present tense) and a few which give *aphethēsetai* (future tense) instead of *apheōntai* (perfect tense), but the best evidence supports *apheōntai.*

one's [sins implied] *you may retain* [*kratēte,* present subjunctive], *they have been retained* [*kekratēntai,* perfect passive indicative]."

We conclude that Matthew 16:19; 18:18; and John 20:23, which, as traditionally rendered, have been considered a stronghold for sacerdotalism, do not support it in any way whatever. There is no foundation anywhere in the New Testament for the claim that the early disciples were given authority to remit and retain sins. We have no record that the apostles or their associates taught people to confess sins to them or that they told people what penance was required to obtain remission of sins. The emphasis of Jesus and the New Testament writers is always upon the gospel which states the conditions required for forgiveness. The conditions are repentance and faith (trust) in the Lord Jesus Christ. Thus salvation is basically a matter between the soul and the Savior. It is not obtained through any human mediator, but only through Christ, the "one mediator between God and men" (I Tim. 2:5).

Professor Mantey says:

During the first three centuries of the Christian Era no one, according to extant writings of the period, ever quoted John 20:23, Matthew 16:19, or 18:18 in favor of sacerdotalism. A thorough study of the Ante-Nicean Fathers reveals that no Greek-writing Church Father ever cited these passages to support such a doctrine.[39]

Quoting once more from Dr. Dayton's article: "It can be concluded that sacerdotalism, as based on these three passages, is highly conjectural grammatically, preposterous logically, impossible theologically, and untenable historically."

---

[39]WPAP, p. 39.

CHAPTER VII

Prepositions

Prepositions constitute one of the most prominent classes of words and provide a prolific area for discriminative study in the Greek New Testament. Because they are involved in exegesis at innumerable points, a knowledge of their nature and function is essential for clarity and accuracy in grasping the message of the biblical text.

Many of the prepositions occur more than a thousand times in the New Testament, and often with varying connotations. Delicate shades of meaning which they express enable the inspired writers to paint linguistic pictures in vivid detail. In many passages the force of prepositions must be examined before an interpreter can deal with exegetical and theological questions. Thus it is only when the student of Greek comprehends the significance of this vital group of terms and their relation to other words in discourse that he is able to appreciate the finer points of syntax.

Greek prepositions, as they appear in the New Testament, are the result of a long and varied history. Originally the case forms of the noun did all the work of expressing word relations. As the language developed, and the various relations between words became too complicated to be expressed by the cases alone, adverbs were enlisted to give more precision to the case ideas. When certain adverbs became fixed in such use, they were treated as a separate part of speech, and became known as prepositions. The word "preposition" is from the Latin *praeponere,* to place before. Hence prepositions commonly stand before the nouns with which they are used, but they may be postpositive.

It is not accurate to say that prepositions and cases "govern" each other. The preposition points up the meaning of a case in a given context where the burden on the case is too heavy for it to bear by itself. In other words, prepositions help to interpret cases. There is an interrelation between the two which amplifies the total idea expressed.

The development of the Greek language from the Homeric to the Attic period was especially marked by the appropriation and use of prepositions. In the Koine era these connectives were employed with great freedom to express many delicate shades of meaning. This is true in particular of the New Testament, where prepositions are used with great frequency.

Prepositions have considerable latitude in Greek syntax, and are not to be limited arbitrarily to a restricted set of meanings. Each preposition has its own etymology and role in the development of the language and is capable of many connotations, depending upon the contexts in which it may be employed.

As integral parts of speech prepositions have basic and regular characteristics which apply to them generally. In addition they have significations apart from their generic features, implicit meanings as well as explicit meanings. What might be supposed to be exceptional meanings of prepositions are quite numerous, as reading in Koine Greek will reveal. It is because a preposition may express several kindred or even diverse ideas that it is difficult at times to ascertain its force in a given passage. The conclusions of many interpreters have been more or less inaccurate because their work was restricted to traditional limited meanings for prepositions. It is fallacious to render a preposition by the same English term in every context, yet one is amazed that the tendency is found so often. Such a procedure ignores the fact that prepositions have root meanings, resultant meanings, and remote meanings; that their force may be local, perfective, or temporal; literal or metaphorical; and that the total idea signified by the preposition, by the case with which it is used and by the relevant context, must be conveyed if an adequate translation is given.

Some mention has already been made of the force of prepositions in composition with verbs. Examples could be multiplied of the vivid pictures thus portrayed, as New Testament illustrations are plentiful. There is the perfective use of *kata* with *ergazomai* in Romans 5:3, "Tribulation *worketh* patience" (*katergazetai,* works effectively, keeps on producing [present tense of linear action] perseverance); in II Corinthians 4:17, "Our light affliction, which is but for a moment, *worketh* [keeps on working out] for us a far more exceeding and eternal weight of glory"; and in 7:10, "The sorrow of the world *worketh* [is now working out and ultimately produces] death." In II Thessalonians 3:11 the preposition *peri* (around) brings out the striking effect of Paul's contrast in the statement, "working not at all, but are busybodies" (not working, but working around, *periergazomenous*); or rendering it more idiomatically, "doing nothing but being busybodies." Again, *ginōskō* means *to know,* and *epiginōskō, to know thoroughly,* while *anaginōskō* is *to read* (cf. *ginōskō* and *anaginōskō* in Acts 8:30). An example of a preposition which has lost its local meaning is the verb *katesthiō, devour* (Matt. 13:4; Mark 4:4). The idea of "downward" has disappeared in this connection, and *kata* brings out the finality of the essential action of the verb.

One of the most common idioms in Koine Greek is the causal use of prepositions—their employment to denote the ground or basis of an idea or action; in such cases they should be translated *because of, by reason of, on account of, owing to, therefore,* and the like. Lexicons, grammars, and commentaries generally are weak in treatments of this significant role of prepositions.[1] Often translators of the New Testament have not indicated clearly that a preposition expressed the basis of an action although the context reflects the causal idea.

By the inductive method an investigator soon learns the large extent to which prepositions have a causal signification in Koine Greek. As one dips into the New Testament, and into the nonbiblical literary monuments of the Imperial period, i.e., the papyri, ostraca, inscriptions, Septuagint, and the literary Koine, he will find many examples of prepositions used in a causal sense.

Of the eighteen classical prepositions, *amphi* does not appear in the New Testament except a few times in composition with verbs. Of the remaining prepositions which occur in their free sense, the writer found fourteen of them employed in a causal

---

[1]An exception to this weakness is the excellent treatment given by Dana and Mantey, *op. cit.,* pp. 96-115.

sense in Koine Greek.[2] The data observed led to the conclusion that the causal signification of prepositions is one of the regular and consistent idioms of Koine syntax. A recognition of this important syntactical feature is an invaluable aid in the translation of the New Testament. Many difficulties of interpretation are solved by an awareness of the causal use of prepositions. Time is well spent when one explores every possibility within the framework of Koine Greek grammar which may lead to a better apprehension of the message of the New Testament.

We shall not mention the instances where the usual renderings reflect the causal force of prepositions, but shall consider several passages where the causal idea is vague or missed entirely although the relevant factors of interpretation call for a causal rendering.

Matthew 3:11

The probability of a causal significance for the preposition *eis* in 3:11 sheds light on John's statement, "I indeed baptize you in water *eis metanoian*." From a grammatical standpoint alone, without regard for the context, since *eis* is often used to denote aim or purpose, *eis metanoian* might be translated "unto repentance." It is thus rendered by Cranmer, King James, Davidson, Rotherham, Syriac, American Standard, Lloyd, Worrell, Godbey, Montgomery. Coverdale, Berry, Darby, Englishman's have "to repentance." Wycliffe has "in to penaunce"; Geneva, "to amendment of life"; Rheims, Arendzen, Campbell-Macknight-Doddridge, "unto penance"; Norton, "that you may reform"; Emphatic Diaglott, "into reformation" (margin, "in order to reformation"); F. S. Ballentine, "to lead you to a change of mind and purpose of heart"; Twentieth Century, "to teach repentance"; Fenton, "preparatory to conversion"; Spencer, "to lead you unto penance."

But the contextual coloring militates against construing *eis* as purposive in this passage. John baptized no one in order to effect penitence; he baptized persons who had already repented and whose lives demonstrated the fruit expressive of repentance (vs. 8). We must conclude that in accord with the

---

[2]For a detailed study of the evidence, reference may be made to the writer's Th.D. dissertation, "The Causal Use of Prepositions in the Greek New Testament."

general teaching and practice of John, he is saying, "I am baptizing you in water *because of* repentance" (vs. 11).

Several versions translate *eis* here with the word "for" which term may reflect the causal idea, inasmuch as one of the recognized dictionary meanings of "for" is motive or cause. (Thus it may be said of a culprit, He was sent to prison *for*, i.e., *on account of*, burglary). "For repentance" is the rendering of Noyes, Moffatt, Weymouth-Robertson, Lamsa, Confraternity, Verkuyl, Letchworth, Revised Standard. Knox says, "I am baptizing you with water, for your repentance"; Riverside, "for a change of heart"; Overbury, "symbolizing the necessity of reformation."

The causal idea is brought out clearly by Tyndale, "I baptize you in water *in token of* repentance"; Goodspeed, *"in token of* repentance"; Weymouth-Hampden-Cook, *"on a profession of* repentance"; Williams, "I am baptizing you in water *to picture* your repentance"; Basic, "Truly, I give baptism with water to those of you who have sorrow for their sins."

The contextual weight seems decisive in favor of a causal translation. Would John preach repentance as a requirement or condition for baptism (vs. 8) and then declare that he was baptizing people in order to produce repentance? Certainly John was consistent. He baptized individuals *eis metanoian, on the basis of repentance.*

The wider context of the Gospels and Acts provides a further commentary on the nature of the baptism performed by John. The recurrent expression *baptisma metanoias* signifies *baptism marked by repentance.* The genitive *metanoias* (the genitive being the case which indicates species or kind) describes the baptism as being characterized by repentance, not as conveying it. As Robertson puts it, John proclaimed "a repentance kind of baptism."[3] In the words of Professor Mantey:

Confirmatory of the necessity of repentance before baptism and consequently also of a causal translation for *eis* in Matthew 3:11 and elsewhere is the expression found four times in the New Testament (Mark 1:4; Luke 3:3; Acts 13:24; 19:4), "a baptism of repentance," which implies, since we have a genitive of description here, a baptism symbolic or expressive of repentance.[4]

[3]RWP, Vol. I, p. 253.
[4]J. R. Mantey, "The Causal Use of *Eis* in the New Testament," *Journal of Biblical Literature*, LXX, Part I, 1951.

Josephus corroborates the Gospel account that John the Baptist required repentance prior to baptism:

> John, who was called the Baptist . . . commanded the Jews to exercise virtue, both as to righteousness towards one another, and piety towards God, and so to come to baptism: for that the washing (baptism) would be acceptable to him, if they made use of it, not in order to the putting away of some sins, but for the purification of the body: *supposing that the soul was thoroughly purified beforehand by righteousness* (*Antiquities of the Jews*, Bk. XVIII. 5.2).[5]

Acts 2:38

Another passage in which the doctrinal issues involved warrant a satisfactory examination is Acts 2:38, in particular the command, "Repent, and let each of you be baptized in the name of Jesus Christ *eis aphesin tōn hamartiōn humōn.*" What does Peter mean by this latter phrase, commonly rendered "for the remission of sins"? Is he teaching that baptism is a condition of salvation, a means of grace? Or does he intend that baptism be understood as a symbol of a transformation already wrought in the heart by the Spirit of God? These questions point up the controversy which has raged long in the history of Christendom between advocates of the idea of salvation by works and exponents of the doctrine of salvation by faith—sacramentalism versus free grace. Inasmuch as these two interpretations are mutually exclusive, and because the nature of the gospel is involved in the basic problem, it is of tremendous importance to interpret correctly the expression of the Apostle.

Here again exegesis hinges largely upon the signification of a preposition. As Peter uses *eis* in this context, is it purposive or causal? A number of translations treat it as purposive. Accordingly, Wycliffe renders the phrase in question, "in to remyssioun of youre synnes"; Campbell-Macknight-Doddridge, "in order to the forgiveness of (your) sins"; Rotherham, "into remission of your sins"; Goodspeed, "in order to have your sins forgiven"; Weymouth-Hampden-Cook, "with a view to the remission of your sins."

Many versions have the rendering "for," including King James, "for the remission of sins"; Revised Standard, "for the forgiveness of your sins"; and "for" is the reading in Tyndale,

[5]William Whiston, *The Works of Josephus*, Vol. III.

Coverdale, Cranmer, Geneva, Rheims, Emphatic Diaglott, Syriac, Englishman's, Darby, Fenton, Moffatt, Riverside, Montgomery, Davidson, Twentieth Century, Noyes, Lamsa, Weymouth-Robertson, Basic, Confraternity, Spencer, Overbury, Lloyd, Verkuyl, Letchworth, Arendzen. F. S. Ballentine has, "Change your mind and the purpose of your heart, and be purified every one of you in the name of Christ for sending away of sins"; American Standard and Godbey, have "unto the remission of your sins." Worrell also has "unto the remission of your sins," but in a footnote he advocates the causal idea when he says:

Be immersed: to show your death, burial, and resurrection with Christ to newness of life (Rom. 6:4; Col. 2:12); not to bring all this about, but to declare your faith in Him, and show by a visible, outward ordinance the change that has been wrought in you already by the Holy Spirit.

Williams' translation interprets *eis* as causal: "Peter said to them, 'You must repent—and, as an expression of it,[6] let everyone of you be baptized in the name of Jesus Christ—that you may have your sins forgiven.' "

Looking at Peter's exhortation in its immediate context, it is clear that baptism is to be preceded by repentance and accompanied by faith in Jesus the Christ as the one who forgives sin. Robertson has called attention to the change of number from plural to singular, and of person from second to third, which marks a break in the thought: *Metanoēsate,* "Repent ye [aorist imperative, second person plural] *kai,* and *baptisthētō,* [aorist imperative passive, third person singular] *let him be baptized* every one of you, etc." "The first thing to do is make a radical and complete change of heart and life. Then let each one be baptized after this change has taken place. . . ."[7]

Meyer says:

The *metanoēsate* demands the change of ethical disposition as the moral condition of being baptized, which directly and necessarily brings with it faith (Mark 1:15); the aorist denotes the immediate accomplishment (cf. 3:19; 8:22), which is conceived as the work of energetic resolution.[8]

---

[6]In a footnote Williams says, "These five words implied from context and usage in the early church."

[7]RWP, Vol. III, p. 34.

[8]Heinrich August Wilhelm Meyer, *Critical and Exegetical Handbook to the Acts of the Apostles,* p. 66.

Alford also understands that Christian baptism is to be "preceded by repentance and accompanied by faith." He says:

The miserable absurdity of rendering *metanoēsate,* or "poenitentiam agite," by "do penance," or understanding it as referring to a course of external rites, is well exposed by this passage—in which the internal change of heart and purpose is insisted on, to be testified by admission into the number of Christ's followers.[9]

The phrase "in the name of Jesus Christ" is also significant. The act of baptism is performed on the confession of the truth which the Name implies, viz., that Jesus is the Christ and the Savior of mankind. The truth denoted by his name is the foundation upon which faith, which expresses itself in baptism, rests. The Apostles baptized individuals who acknowledged Jesus as Lord, and such acknowledgment implies repentance and faith.

It should be remembered that the causal use of *eis* is just as grammatical in some contexts as is the purposive use of *eis* in other contexts. There can be no question that *eis to kērugma Iōna* (Matt. 12:41; Luke 11:32) means *because of the preaching of Jonah.* It is the only interpretation allowed by the context. The Ninevites did not repent for the purpose of getting Jonah to preach; they repented on account of his proclamation. As D. L. Cooper has observed, in this type of context the retrospective idea is favored rather than the prospective, so that *eis* has "a backward look."[10] Robertson has pointed out that causal *eis* "is just as good Greek" as purposive *eis,* and says "illustrations of both usages are numerous in the New Testament and the Koine generally."[11]

In the larger context of New Testament soteriology as a whole, repentance and faith precede baptism (cf. Acts 8:36 f.; 9:5-18; 10:47; Mark 16:16). No passage is found in which baptism is mentioned as a sacrament having saving efficacy. In a number of passages the condition for salvation is stated to be repentance, with no mention of baptism (cf. Mark 6:12; Luke 13:3; 24:47; Acts 3:19; 17:30; 26:20; II Cor. 7:9 f.; II Pet. 3:9). Therefore it seems clear that definite spiritual conditions

[9]Henry Alford, *The Greek Testament,* Vol. II, pp. 24, 25.
[10]David Lipscomb Cooper, "The Use of *En* and *Eis* in the New Testament and the Contemporaneous Nonliterary Papyri," p. 130.
[11]RWP, Vol. III, p. 35.

are to precede and prepare the way for baptism. This is the message of Peter in Acts 2:38. Robertson says:

> My view is decidedly against the idea that Peter, Paul, or any one in the New Testament taught baptism as essential to the remission of sins or the means of securing such remission. So I understand Peter to be urging baptism on each of them who had already turned (repented) and for it to be done in the name of Jesus Christ on the basis of the forgiveness of sins which they had already received.[12]

Romans 4:20

Although the natural circumstances were not conducive to faith that a child could be born to Abraham and Sarah in their old age, God promised them a son, and on the basis of that promise the patriarch had faith.

King James says, "He staggered not *at* [*eis*] the promise of God through unbelief." And "at" is also the rendering of Tyndale, Syriac, Cranmer, Weymouth, Godbey, Williams, Englishman's, Berry, Knox, Darby, Overbury, Lloyd, Letchworth, F. S. Ballentine. Moffatt and Verkuyl read "about"; American Standard, "looking unto"; Spencer, "looking to"; Rotherham and Davidson, "with respect to"; Noyes, "in respect to"; Montgomery, "with regard to"; Revised Standard, "concerning"; Emphatic Diaglott margin, Geneva, Campbell-Macknight-Doddridge, "against"; Arendzen, Riverside, Coverdale, Rheims, Wycliffe, "in"; Fenton, "Nor did he doubtingly criticize the promise of God"; Basic, "Still, he did not give up faith in the undertaking of God"; Twentieth Century, "He was not led by want of faith to doubt God's promise"; Lamsa, "He did not doubt the promise of God as one who lacks faith"; Goodspeed, "He did not incredulously question God's promise."

The meaning of the passage is more luminous and the faith of Abraham is emphasized with reference to its basis by taking *eis* in a causal sense which seems implied by the context. The clear causal idea is brought out by Worrell, "In view of the promise of God, he wavered not through unbelief"; Confraternity, "In view of the promise of God, he did not waver"; and by Professor Mantey, "Abraham, being about one hundred years old, took into consideration his own deadened body and

---

[12]*Ibid.*, p. 36.

the deadness of Sarah's womb, but on account of the promise
of God he did not waver in unbelief."[13]

Romans 11:32

Paul's statement in Romans 11:32a constitutes a difficult
theological problem when the preposition *eis* is interpreted as
denoting aim or purpose; e.g., American Standard, Worrell,
"For God hath shut up all *unto* disobedience"; Revised Standard, "For God has consigned all men to disobedience"; Noyes,
F. S. Ballentine, Moffatt also have "to." By taking *eis* in the
purposive sense the Apostle's assertion would imply that
human sin has a positive relation to the act and intent of God.
But as Denny has pointed out,[14] it would be erroneous to draw
such an inference from the concrete historical problem before
Paul (viz., the status of Jew and Gentile in the development of
God's way of salvation), and to apply it to the general abstract
question of the relation of the human will to the divine will.

It seems that the proper interpretation is to take *eis* as causal.
Paul's argument is that salvation is by grace to all men alike on
the basis of faith, that no people have any merit of their own.
Both Jews and Gentiles (*tous pantas*, them all) are in need of
grace as both alike have transgressed the divine law, and God
has concluded them all under condemnation *on account of*
disobedience.

Robertson interprets *eis* as causal in this context. He says
sunekleisen (shut up together, completely) is "a resultant
(effective) aorist, *because of* the disbelief and disobedience of
both Gentile (1:17-32) and Jew (2:1—3:20)."[15]

Titus 3:14

A number of interesting ideas are reflected in the various
renderings of Titus 3:14. Just what is Paul saying here? In
particular, what is the force of the preposition *eis* in his exhortation?

King James translates the passage, "And let ours also learn
to maintain good works *for* necessary uses, that they be not
unfruitful"; Campbell-Macknight-Doddridge, "And let ours

---

[13]J. R. Mantey, "The Causal Use of *Eis* in the New Testament." *Journal of Biblical Literature*, LXX, Part I, 1951.
[14]James Denny, EGT, Vol. II, p. 685.
[15]RWP, Vol. IV, p. 399f.

also learn to practise honest trades for necessary uses"; American Standard (mg. "wants"), Godbey, Arendzen, "for necessary uses." Worrell, Darby, Davidson, Englishman's, Noyes, read "for necessary wants." Williams has, "to meet the necessary demands"; Overbury, "so as to supply necessary needs"; Confraternity, "in order to meet cases of necessity"; Spencer, "so as to help urgent needs"; Revised Standard, "so as to help cases of urgent need"; Tyndale, Coverdale, "as nede requyreth"; Rotherham, "for needful services"; Twentieth Century, "so as to meet the most pressing needs"; Riverside, "so as to be able to meet pressing needs"; Goodspeed, "so as to meet these pressing demands"; Verkuyl, "to meet the requisite needs"; Fenton, "so that they may not be indifferent towards those who are in want"; Lloyd, Basic, "for necessary purposes." Lamsa has, "And let our people be taught to do good works in times of emergency"; Syriac, "on occasions of emergency"; Moffatt, "so as to be able to meet such special occasions"; F. S. Ballentine, "for the relief of those in want"; Weymouth-Robertson, "And let our people too learn to follow honest occupations for the supply of their necessities." Montgomery, quoting the translation of Arthur S. Way, has a different idea, " 'Let our people learn to devote themselves to honest work to supply the necessities of their teachers.' "

The translation suggested by Professor Mantey, interpreting the preposition *eis* in a causal sense, reflects a deeper meaning in the admonition of Paul and emphasizes one of the great principles of the Christian life, viz., that individuals who are saved by grace express their faith by their works. Dr. Mantey renders this verse, "Let our people learn to maintain good works *because of* the compelling need (for them) in order that they may not be unfruitful."[16]

Hebrews 12:7

The form *hupomenete* may be the present active indicative, or it may be the imperative. If it is taken as the indicative, and if *eis* is interpreted as causal, the phrase *eis paideian hupomenete*, which our Greek text sets off as a complete sentence, may be translated, "Because of discipline you are enduring."

---

[16]J. R. Mantey, "The Causal Use of *Eis* in the New Testament."

The variant reading (found only in a few minuscules) which has the conditional particle *ei* instead of the better attested *eis* is reflected in some translations. King James reads, "*If* ye endure chastening," and "if" is the rendering also in Tyndale, Coverdale, Cranmer, Geneva, Campbell-Macknight-Doddridge, Worrell, Fenton, Englishman's, Emphatic Diaglott, Letchworth.

A number take *hupomenete* as imperative. Thus Wycliffe, "Abide ye still in chastisynge"; Rotherham, "For the sake of discipline, persevere"; Spencer, "Endure suffering as a discipline"; Syriac, "Therefore endure ye the chastisement"; Verkuyl, "You must endure for the sake of correction"; Knox, "Be patient, then, while correction lasts"; Lloyd, "Endure unto chastisement"; Rheims, "Perseuere ye in discipline"; Lamsa, "Now therefore, endure chastisement"; Godbey, "Endure unto chastisement"; Williams, "You must submit to discipline"; Goodspeed, "You must submit to it as discipline"; Confraternity, "Continue under discipline."

Others take the verb as indicative. So Noyes, American Standard, "It is for chastening that ye endure"; Davidson, "Unto chastening ye are enduring"; Darby, "Ye endure for chastening"; Weymouth, "The sufferings that you are enduring are for your discipline"; Moffatt, Revised Standard, "It is for discipline that you have to endure"; Riverside, "that you are enduring"; Montgomery, "It is for discipline that you are enduring these sufferings"; Twentieth Century, "It is for your discipline that you have to endure all this."

It is grammatically correct to interpret *eis* in a purposive sense, as reflected in the foregoing renderings, if the context so indicates. But it should be remembered also that causal *eis* is one of the consistent idioms of Koine syntax and is the best interpretation in certain contexts. The passage under consideration seems to have a more significant meaning if *eis* is translated causally. Professor Mantey thus translates verses 6-7a, "For the Lord disciplines him whom he loves, and chastises every son whom he receives. It is *because of* discipline that you are enduring."[17]

---
[17]*Loc. cit.*

"Eis Onoma," in the Name

Jesus says:

He that receiveth a prophet in the name of a prophet shall receive a prophet's reward; and he that receiveth a righteous man in the name of a righteous man shall receive a righteous man's reward. And whosoever shall give to drink unto one of these little ones a cup of cold water only in the name of a disciple, verily I say unto you, he shall in no wise lose his reward (Matt. 10:41-42).

The connotation of *onoma* (name) is very interesting and significant. The name of an individual denotes the person, or the essence of what he is. A great deal of light has been shed on the expression *eis to onoma* by the papyri, inscriptions, and ostraca. According to Heitmuller it has been found at times without the genitive, in the sense of "to the name," i.e., "to the dignity or honor"; and he found a parallel in an oath from the Herodian period, "to swear into the name" of someone.[18] This is parallel to the New Testament phrase, "to baptize into the name."

Deissmann refers to an ostracon from Thebes, of the second century A.D., from his own collection, containing the formula (so common that it is abbreviated) *eis onom* (a). It is part of an order to an official of a state granary to transfer wheat to another person's account,[19] and shows that *eis onoma* signified "into his possession." In those days, as at the present time, the property of an individual was that which belonged to his name or was registered to his account.

Heitmuller sums up the results of his investigation of the phrase in nonbiblical Greek as follows:

Eis to onoma tinos[20] as the objective of the verb or sentence was a formula very frequently in use in the Hellenistic worldspeech; in the vernacular, especially the business speech, it was current long before the rise of the New Testament; into the literary language, as it appears, it later came up; it indicates the *dedication to a person,* the presentation of an object in the relation of *ownership;* it is to be noted thereby that *onoma* in the formula has not lost its essential meaning.[21]

In the New Testament this vital signification of *onoma* is

[18]Wilhelm Heitmuller, *Im Namen Jesu,* p. 101.
[19]Adolf Deissmann, *Light from the Ancient East,* p. 121.
[20]Meaning "in the name of anyone."
[21]Heitmuller, *op. cit.,* p. 109.

reflected in its use with prominent verbs like *pisteuō,* to believe, and *baptizō,* to baptize. With *pisteuō* in this connection three prepositions are used, *en, epi,* and *eis. En* with the locative case indicates the sphere within which an action takes place. Thus, when one believes *in* Christ, the idea is that the faith of the believer is centered in the Lord. Such a person is no longer self-centered. He thinks within a new and different frame of reference. *Epi* with *pisteuō* indicates that the believer's faith is *upon* the Christ—trusting him as Savior. And as already noted, *eis to onoma* is significant. With the verb *pisteuō* this formula has a profound meaning. The Hellenistic world in the first Christian century was familiar with the expression *eis to onoma* as a technical idiom which signified the transfer of property. The masses who listened to the apostles proclaim the gospel had been accustomed to seeing slaves bought by pagan temples "into the name" of one or another local deity. When they heard the formula associated with *pisteuō,* to believe, to trust, and *Iēsous,* Jesus, they would understand readily that "believing into the name of Jesus" means ceasing to be the property or slave of the god of this world and becoming the possession and servant of the Lord, a glorious transformation indeed!

This idiom is used also with *baptizō* in passages like Matthew 28:19; Acts 8:16; 19:5. We are not only to believe into the name of the Lord Jesus Christ; we are to be baptized into the name of the Lord. This expression, according to the well-known formula of the Imperial period, means that a baptized believer is publicly marked as belonging to God. Deissmann cites an inscription dating from the beginning of the Imperial period which contains the expression *ktēmatōnai eis to tou theou* (Zeus) *onoma* which he is certain presupposes the same conception of the term *onoma* which is found used in a Christian sense. Deissmann concludes:

> Just as, in the Inscription, *to buy into the name of God* means to buy so that the article bought belongs to God, so also the idea underlying, e.g., the expressions *to baptize into the name of the Lord,* or *to believe into the name of the Son of God,* is that baptism or faith constitutes the belonging to God or to the Son of God.[22]

---

[22]Adolf Deissmann, *Bible Studies,* p. 146 f.

Robertson[23] mentions an Oxyrhynchus papyrus (37, dated A.D. 49) in which the expression *onomati eleutherou* (in the name of freedom) means "in virtue of being free born."

Thus it is clear that in Matthew 10:41-42 Jesus means, "He who receives a prophet *as such* [on the basis that he is indeed a prophet] ... a righteous man *because* he is a righteous man ... a disciple *by virtue of* his character as such shall have his appropriate reward." The causal idea is prominent. " 'He that receiveth a prophet from no ulterior motive, but simply *qua* prophet would receive a reward in the coming age equal to that of his guest' (McNeile)."[24] The ethical concern is supreme in the mind of Jesus.

Translations which render *eis onoma* "in the name of" include Wycliffe, Tyndale, Coverdale, Cranmer, Geneva, Rheims, King James, Davidson, Darby, Syriac, F. S. Ballentine, Worrell,[25] American Standard, Godbey, Basic, Englishman's, Lamsa, Arendzen. Rotherham has "into a prophet's name ... into a righteous one's name ... into a disciple's name"; Emphatic Diaglott, "in a name of"; Williams, "as a prophet ... as such ... because"; and *eis onoma* is rendered "because" by Campbell-Macknight-Doddridge, Norton, Noyes, Lloyd, Twentieth Century, Fenton, Riverside, Emphatic Diaglott, margin, Montgomery, Weymouth, Moffatt, Goodspeed, Spencer, Verkuyl, Knox, Overbury, Confraternity, Revised Standard, Letchworth.

In Matthew 18:5; Mark 9:37; Luke 9:48 there is a similar idiom with the preposition *epi*. The causal idea is prominent as with *eis* in Matthew 10:41-42. It is clear that *epi tōi onomati mou* means "on the basis or ground of my name," "because of me," "on account of what I am and who I am," "by my authority." "Name" is that by which Jesus or God is known and it may denote his revelation.

"Huper" in I Corinthians 15:29

A perplexing problem for New Testament exegetes has been Paul's expression, *baptizomenoi huper tōn nekrōn* (I Cor.

---

[23]RWP, Vol. I, p. 85.

[24]*Loc. cit.*

[25]In a footnote Worrell says, *"Receives a prophet;* because of love for Jesus Christ and for His servants."

15:29). More than thirty interpretations, representing various theological views, have been suggested for this passage.

The English translations generally cling to the traditional renderings for the preposition *huper*. Accordingly the phrase is rendered "baptized *for* the dead" by Wycliffe, Geneva, Rheims, King James, Noyes, Englishman's, Syriac, American Standard, Darby, Godbey, Riverside, Weymouth, Knox, Montgomery, Basic, Verkuyl, Lamsa, Confraternity, Arendzen. Worrell has "immersed for" (margin, "on behalf of"), and "on behalf of" is the rendering of Emphatic Diaglott, Davidson, Twentieth Century, Lloyd, Moffatt, Goodspeed, Overbury, Williams, Revised Standard. Rotherham has "in behalf of"; Fenton, "for the sake of"; and Campbell-Macknight-Doddridge paraphrase it, "immersed for the resurrection of the dead." F. S. Ballentine gives an interpretive rendering, "If the dead are not raised at all, why then are they purified for such an end?"

Some take *huper* in a local sense, "baptized over the dead." Tyndale, Coverdale, Cranmer, and Luther, along with others, held such a view, i.e., that "over the dead" meant over their sepulchers. But Alford[26] rejects such an interpretation, arguing that *huper* is not used in the local sense in the New Testament.

We are sure that the Pauline expression does not indicate any sort of vicarious baptism; i.e., a baptism performed upon living persons to convey benefits to the dead. The New Testament nowhere teaches such a doctrine.

One of the function of *huper* in Koine Greek is to denote the cause, basis, or ground of an action. There are illustrations of the causal use of this preposition in the Septuagint (cf. I Chron. 29:9; Jer. 19:8) and examples have been found in the papyri[27] and in Josephus.[28] In the New Testament where *huper* is often used to signify "for the sake of" or "in behalf of" (cf. Acts 15:26; 21:13; III John 7), there is sometimes a causal idea inferred in the construction. The idea of doing something "for the sake of" an individual or thing may involve also the notion "because of." This dual concept is implied in Paul's statement in Ephesians 6:20, inasmuch as the gospel is both the object and the cause for which the Apostle is bound.

---

[26]Henry Alford, *The Greek Testament.*
[27]E.g., P. Tebt., Part I.50.18; P. Ryl. 113.23; 153.25; P. Oxy., Part VIII.1124.4.
[28]Vol. IV, *Jewish Antiquities*, II.41.

Note the same dual thought with *huper* in II Thessalonians 1:5. Such a twofold idea is reflected also in a number of passages regarding sacrifices for sin (cf. Heb. 5:1; 7:27; 9:7; 10:12). There is a clear causal use of *huper* in Romans 15:9, "And that the Gentiles might glorify God *because of* (his) mercy." There is adequate grammatical basis for placing the phrase "baptized for the dead" in this same category.

Many problems are solved by interpreting *huper* causally in I Corinthians 15:29. Other renderings for this preposition are unsatisfactory here in the light of the general context of Pauline theology. A causal interpretation is in harmony with the general tenor of the New Testament as well as being one of the recognized uses of *huper* in Koine Greek. There is strong logic for translating Paul's statement, "baptized because of the dead" inasmuch as the death of Christians frequently leads to the conversion of their survivors. It is a well-attested fact of history that the exhortations of dying Christians have often constrained loved ones to receive the Christ. Findlay says, "The hope of future blessedness, allying itself with family affections and friendship, was one of the most powerful factors in the early spread of Christianity."[29] Could not Paul designate such converts "baptized because of the dead" inasmuch as they became Christians through the influence of their beloved dead? Findlay holds this view and remarks, "The obscure passage has, upon this explanation, a large, abiding import suitable to the solemn and elevated context in which it stands."[30]

---

[29]G. G. Findlay, EGT, Vol. II, p. 931.
[30]*Loc. cit.*

CHAPTER VIII

Participles

Participles are verbal adjectives. As its name implies the participle shares (takes part, participates) in the nature of both a verb and an adjective, as the infinitive shares in the characteristics of both verb and noun. And, like the infinitive, the participle expresses nonfinite, undefined action.

Being adjectives, participles have gender, number, and case in which respects they agree with the nouns that they modify. Also, being verbs, participles have tense and voice, receive adverbial modifiers, and may be transitive or intransitive (may or may not take a direct object).

The tense and temporal implications of participles are the most important aspects for our brief study here. Tense in the participle has the same significance it does in the finite modes; that is, tense expresses kind of action, or the state of the action. The aorist participle denotes punctiliar action; the present participle denotes linear or incompleted action. For example, in Hebrews 6: 10 there is *diakonēsantes* (aorist, *having served*) and *diakonountes* (present, *continuing to serve*). The perfect participle accents the idea of completion and the results of an action, as *kekopiakōs* in John 4: 6 which pictures Jesus in a state of weariness as a result of his journey. In Galatians 4: 3, Paul uses the perfect passive participle *dedoulōmenoi* to indicate the pre-Christian experience of enslavement in a state of bondage. In Paul's prayer for the Ephesians, he asks that God give them the spirit of wisdom and revelation in the knowledge of him, that the eyes of their heart might be *in a state of enlightenment* (*pephōtismenous,* perfect passive participle). Perfect passive participles in I Timothy 6: 5 describe the condition of men who are *corrupted* in mind and *destitute* of the truth. In Ephesians 4: 18-19 are two periphrastic perfect passive participles and one perfect participle which describe the sad condition of individuals who have hardened their hearts against God: *having become darkened* (*eskotōmenoi*) in understanding, *having become alienated* (*apēllotriōmenoi*) from the life of God, and *having reached a point where they cease to feel compunction* (*apēlgēkotes*), they continue in their sad state.

The significance of the periphrastic future perfect passive participles in Matthew 16:19 and 18:18, fraught with such far-reaching soteriological implications, were treated in the chapter on Tense.

Greek participles do not convey independent expressions of time, but in relation to their contexts they usually have a temporal significance. The temporal force of the participle is relative to the time of the principal verb of the sentence. In other words, a participle gets its time from the verb with which it is used. Thus, as suggested by its context, the participle may indicate (a) antecedent action (usually expressed by the aorist or perfect), (b) coincident or simultaneous action (usually expressed by the present, though it may also be expressed by the aorist participle), and (c) subsequent action (regularly expressed by the future participle). The context must be noted in order to ascertain how a participle is used in a given instance.

The most common participles are the present and the aorist, the former being used with more latitude than the latter. "The action of the present participle may precede (antecedent), coincide with (simultaneous), or follow (subsequent) the action of the principal verb." "The action of the aorist participle may be antecedent to, or simultaneous with, that of the principal verb."[1]

Machen says that as a general rule the present participle expresses contemporary action, and the aorist participle expresses action prior to that of the leading verb.[2] When a Greek present participle is translated by a temporal clause in English, the temporal clause is usually introduced by *while*. When a

[1]William Hersey Davis op. cit., p. 104.
[2]J. Gresham Machen, *New Testament Greek for Beginners*, p. 206. Machen also points out that the aorist participle is sometimes used to denote the same act as the leading verb; e.g., the expression common in the Gospels, "Jesus answered and said" (*the answering*, aorist participle, being identical action with the saying). But Machen says, "And it is exceedingly important that this idiom should not be allowed to obscure the fact that in the majority of cases the aorist participle denotes action prior to the time of the leading verb" (p. 207).

Greek aorist participle is translated by a temporal clause, the temporal clause is usually introduced by *when* or *after*.

There are many examples of the distinction between present and aorist participles. In Acts 13:2, two present participles indicate contemporary action, *while they were ministering . . . while they were fasting;* and in verse 3, three aorist participles express antecedent action, *having fasted, having prayed, having placed upon* them hands. Linear action is indicated by the present participle *epikaloumenous, those continuing to call upon* the name of the Lord (Acts 9:14). And the same force is seen in Paul's powerful statement, "I can do all things through Christ which *strengtheneth (endunamounti, keeps empowering)* me" (Phil. 4:13). The participle is from the word *dunamis* (basis of our word *dynamite*). Williams gives as the literal rendering for this verse, "I have power for all things through Him who puts a dynamo in me."

The Acts is plentiful with examples of the aorist participle in contexts which indicate antecedent action; e.g., *"having come together"* (1:6); "the Holy Spirit *having come* upon you" (1:8); *"having been scattered"* (11:19); *"having been sent forth"* (13:4); *"having come down* from Judea" (15:1); *"having traveled through* Amphipolis and Apollonia, they came to Thessalonica" (17:1); "Paul, *having passed through* the highlands, came to Ephesus and finding certain disciples, he asked them if they had received the Holy Spirit, *having believed"* (19:1-2); *"having come* to us, and *having taken* Paul's belt, *having bound* his own feet and hands" (21:11). Note also 9:18, "and *having arisen* [i.e., after he arose], he was baptized." These examples are like Mark 16:20, *"having gone out* [meaning *after they had gone forth*], they preached.

Washing Away Sins

According to Acts 9:1-17, Saul of Tarsus was converted on the Damascus Road. Why, then, does Ananias seemingly say to him (22:16), "Arise, and be baptized, and wash away thy sins, *calling on* the Lord's name"? (King James, English Revised, American Standard, Godbey, Goodspeed, Confraternity, Revised Standard; *calling upon,* Weymouth, Montgomery; *invoking his name,* Moffatt). Such a rendering implies baptismal regeneration, but the general teaching of the New Testament is that salvation is by faith in the atonement of Christ, apart from participation in any ritual or ceremony. Although the New Testament calls upon believers to be baptized, baptism there always follows repentance and faith; i.e., immersion is an ordinance for regenerate persons, being an outward symbol of inward experience.

The tense of the participle rendered "calling on" clears up the problem. It is *epikalesamenos,* aorist participle, and taking it as indicating antecedent action, which is the common significance of the aorist, the normal translation would be "having called upon" the Lord's name. The calling upon the name of the Lord took place before the invitation to baptism. Inasmuch as Paul had already called upon the Savior's name, he was a proper candidate for baptism. So here, as elsewhere in the New Testament, immersion pictures the spiritual transformation already experienced by a believer. Thus Acts 22:16 is in harmony with the account of Paul's regeneration as recorded in Acts 9, and with the New Testament doctrine of salvation by grace through faith.

The idea of baptismal remission is no problem when it is understood in the figurative sense, as mentioned in I Peter 3:21. Baptism signifies a social absolving of sins as it pictures the new life (death, burial, resurrection) of the believer. But it can never actually wash away sins. "The saving by baptism which Peter here mentions is only symbolic (a metaphor or picture as in Romans 6:2-6), not actual as Peter hastens to explain."[3]

It is regrettable that some commentators and preachers draw erroneous inferences and become dogmatic about passages which they do not really understand. Their sincerity is not doubted; nevertheless they have constructed doctrinal positions for which there is no scriptural foundation. How refreshing to read the interpretation of a scholar like Robertson who knew so well what the Greek text means: "Here [Acts 22:16] baptism pictures the change that had already taken place when Paul surrendered to Jesus on the way (vs. 10). Baptism here pictures the washing away of sins by the blood of Christ."[4]

[3]RWP, Vol. VI, p. 119.
[4]RWP, Vol. III, p. 392.

Any Hope for Backsliders?

Some Bible students have concluded that Hebrews 6:4-6 allows no hope for the reclamation of backsliders. The reason assumed for the impossibility of renewal is the statement as rendered: "Seeing they crucify to themselves the Son of God afresh, and put him to an open shame" (KJV, ASV, English Revised).

It must be recognized that a person, because he is a free moral agent, might fall and fall away utterly into such total apostasy as to preclude the possibility of renewal. Sometimes we hear it said that upon such an individual the powers of grace have been exhausted. Rather, it should be stated that the apostate has reached a point of obduracy where he no longer responds to the call of grace. The correspondence between such a state and the consequence of the blasphemy against the Holy Spirit suggests itself at once (cf. Matt. 12:31; Mark 3:29; Luke 12:10). There is, therefore, a relapse for which there is no restoration. It is the ultimate, final rejection of the only power by which reclamation could be effected. Even the love of God, revealed in the sacrifice of Jesus Christ for the salvation of the world, is scornfully dismissed or ridiculed. When men insult God, contemptuously regard his Son, and grieve the Holy Spirit, there is no remaining hope for them.

The context of Hebrews 6:6, seen in the light of the epistle, indicates that the defection meant by the author is a practical abandonment of Christianity and return to former traditions. Many persons did leave the faith and return to Judaism or gave in to the threats of paganism in the early period of persecution. Thus their practical conduct was like those who actually crucified the Savior.

On the other hand, the passage has led some Christians to despair of salvation, although they were desirous of it, under the idea that they had sinned away their day of grace. It may be said that the very state of mind of persons who are beset of such fears is an indication they are not of those described by the text. They cannot have fallen entirely from the orbit of redeeming grace if they have the inclination to repent and to experience forgiveness. Greek syntax offers hope, even in Hebrews 6:6. The temporal force of the two present participles, *anastaurountas, w h i l e crucifying,* and *paradeigmatizontas, while putting (Him) to open shame,* implies that if persons guilty of such sin will cease it, and repent, they can be reclaimed. Arthur S. Way renders the passage:

> It is a task beyond human powers to go on indefinitely rekindling in them the new life-purpose, so long as they go on re-crucifying, in His relation to them, the Son of God, and continue to bring public opprobrium on His Name.

Salvation Involves Crisis and Continuous Trust

In the chapter on Tense it was pointed out that redemption involves both the initial act of believing in (receiving) Jesus Christ and the continuous attitude of commitment to him. This dual aspect of salvation is illustrated often by the force of participles. The following are some examples:

"He came unto his own [*ta idia,* neuter plural, *his own things*], and his own [*hoi idioi,* masculine plural, *his own people*] received him not. But as many as *received* [*elabon,* aorist indicative, emphasizing one definite act] him, to them gave he power [*exousian, authority,* liberty of action] to become the sons of God, even to *them that believe* [*pisteuousin,* present participle, *those who continue trusting*] on his name" (John 1:11-12).

The durative idea reflected by the present tense is seen in John 3:14-16, "And as Moses lifted up the serpent in the wilderness, even so must the Son of man be lifted up: that whosoever *believeth* [*pisteuōn,* present participle, *goes on trusting*] in him should not perish, but *have* [*echēi,* present subjunctive, *might continue to have*] eternal life. For God so loved the world, that he gave his only begotten Son, that whosoever *believeth* [*pisteuōn,* present participle, *goes on trusting*] in him should not perish, but *have* [*echēi, might go on having*] everlasting life."

Eternal life is not merely a matter of endless existence; it is a quality of life, the God-kind of life. All men, by their very nature, are immortal. Likewise Satan and the demons have endless existence. The New Testament does not equate never-ending being with eternal life. Only Christians, that is, individuals who have received Jesus Christ and are trusting in him, have eternal life, because it is experienced by faith. It is redemption through and fellowship with the Son of God and with the Father. Our Lord defines it in John 17:3: "And this is life eternal, that they might know thee the only true God, and Jesus Christ, whom thou hast sent." So eternal life begins here and now for the believer, continues beyond the experience of death, and will bring us ultimately into the heavenly dimensions of reality in eternity.

The linear idea of saving faith is emphasized in John 3:36, "He that *believeth* [*pisteuōn*, present participle, *goes on trusting*] on the Son *hath* [*echei*, present indicative, *continues to have*] everlasting life." The believer in Christ has this life the moment he believes, and as long as he believes. If it were impossible under any circumstances for a person to backslide, probation for him would be meaningless. This is not to say that it is necessary to backslide. By faith the believer enters a state of righteousness where he remains as long as he is *the trusting one.*

Jesus says (John 5:24): "Verily, verily, I say unto you, He that *heareth* [present participle] my word, and *believeth* [present participle, *goes on trusting*] on him that sent me, *hath* [*echei*, present tense, *goes on having*] everlasting life, and shall not come into condemnation; but *is passed from* [*metabebēken*, perfect tense, *is in the state of having passed from*] death unto life."

John 3:18 is illuminating: *"The one who continues trusting* [*pisteuōn*, present participle] in him is not condemned; *the one who does not continue trusting* [same construction but with negative particle] *is already condemned* [perfect passive, *is in a state of condemnation*] because *he has not believed with abiding results* [*pepisteuken*, perfect tense, indicating permanent attitude of unbelief] in the name of the only Son of God." Contrast this passage with Acts 16:34 where the experience of the Philippian jailer is described with the perfect active participle *pepisteukōs, having come to faith and abiding in a state of trust.*

Paul says in Romans 3:22: "Indeed, God's kind of righteousness is through faith in Jesus Christ, operative in all who *continue trusting* [*pisteuontas*, present participle of linear action]." He says in I Corinthians 1:21, "It pleased God by the foolishness of preaching *to save* [*sōsai*, aorist infinitive, viewing the process in its entirety] *them that believe.*" (The present participle emphasizes the habit of faith; to have believed at one time is not enough.)

In verse 18, two present passive participles denote two processes going on: "For the preaching of the cross is to them that *perish* [*apollumenois, those who are perishing*] foolishness; but unto us which are *saved* [*sōzomenois, being saved*] it is the power of God." Paul's two basic categories here include all mankind. Each of us is in one of two classes of people: those who are perishing or those who are being saved.

There is initial salvation and ultimate salvation. Every person who believes in Christ has eternal life—has it now, has it while and as long as he goes on trusting. Thus we see the importance of Jesus' statement, "He that endureth to the end shall be saved [ultimate salvation]" (Matt. 10:22). In this light the Apostle John writes, "And these things *stand written* [*gegraptai,* perfect tense] in order that *ye might continue believing* [present subjunctive] that Jesus is the Christ the Son of God, and in order that *continuing to believe* [present participle] *ye might go on having* [present subjunctive] life in his name" (John 20:31).

CHAPTER IX

Conjunctions

Conjunctions are connectives which link together sentences, clauses, phrases, or words. Robertson calls them "the joints of speech."[1] A conjunction may serve merely as a copula, or along with its connective function it may give additional meaning to words preceding or following it.[2]

Unlike our English connectives, a Greek conjunction may have a number of meanings, depending upon its context. Therefore each Greek conjunction requires careful contextual study in order that its precise significance may be ascertained.

There are some twenty-four different conjunctions in the Greek New Testament. Students will wish to make a comprehensive study of them all and may refer to the New Testament Greek grammars for complete lists and classifications. Here only a few conjunctions have been considered.

Ara

Studies in the Koine have demonstrated a greater latitude in the use of conjunctions than was realized formerly. For example, it is now clear that the conjunction *ara* was employed not only in an inferential sense meaning *therefore, wherefore, accordingly, consequently, then, so,* which was its usual function, but that it was sometimes employed as an emphatic particle meaning *certainly, indeed, really, actually.* For example, in Matthew 7:20 *arage* (*ara* plus the intensive particle *ge*) is emphatic, "*Certainly* you will recognize them by their fruits." *Ara* adds force to Peter's exhortation to Simon the Sorcerer (Acts 8:22): "Repent therefore of this thy wickedness, and pray God, if perhaps [*ara,* indeed] the thought of thine heart may be forgiven thee." In 11:18, this conjunction shows the

---

[1]R, p. 1177.
[2]D-M, p. 239.

excitement and submission of the critics of Peter when they exclaimed, "Then [*ara*, indeed, of a truth] hath God also to the Gentiles granted repentance unto life." Here *ara* is all the more emphatic as it stands at the beginning of a clause. The common inferential idea is too weak here (cf. "then" in King James, English Revised, American Standard, Godbey, Goodspeed, Revised Standard, and others), but Moffatt is forceful, " 'So God has *actually* allowed the Gentiles to repent and live!' " Other examples of the emphatic use of *ara* include II Corinthians 1:17, where Paul says, "I did not *actually* use fickleness, did I?"; and Hebrews 12:8, "Now if you are without discipline, of which all have become partakers, you are *actually* illegitimate children and not sons." Compare Acts 12:18 where the use of *ara* reflects the astonishment of the soldiers as they wondered what *really* had become of Peter.

Along with the intensive particle *ge*, the emphatic force of *ara*, has an illuminating connotation in Phillip's approach to the Ethiopian, "Do you *really* understand what you are reading?" (Acts 8:30). Philip's question was more courteous than it would have been without the use of *ara*. A number of renderings, including King James, English Revised, American Standard, Goodspeed, Montgomery, Weymouth, Williams, Revised Standard, do not indicate the force of *ara* in this passage, but Moffatt does. In fact, many translations are weak with respect to conjunctions generally. Often conjunctions are rendered inadequately or not translated at all. This weakness is especially prominent in the Revised Standard Version which considers conjunctions as redundant in many passages.

Gar

Another interesting conjunction is *gar*, which is a compound of *ge* and *ara*. Like *ara* its most frequent use is inferential or illative, introducing a reason. Of this there are numerous examples. The Son of Mary is to be called Jesus, "*for* [*gar*] he shall save his people from their sins" (Matt. 1:21); Paul is fond of *gar* in this sense. Compare Romans 1:9, 11, 16, 17, 18, 20.

There are a number of instances where *gar* is used in an explanatory sense. Note "*for* they were fishers" (Matt. 4:18); "*for* she was of the age of twelve years" (Mark 5:42); "*for* it [the stone] was very great" (16:4); "*for* his disciples were gone away unto the city to buy meat" (John 4: 8) ; *"for instance* [or now] which of you desiring to build a tower" (Luke 14: 28) ; *"now* it stands written in the law of Moses" (I Cor. 9: 9). We might render Romans 7: 2, "A wife, *for example,* remains bound by law to her husband."

Then there are many passages in which the contexts call for an emphatic translation for *gar.* In Acts 4: 34, the first *gar* is emphatic and the second one is explanatory: *"In fact,* no one among them was in want, *for* as many as were owners of estates or houses were selling and bringing, etc." *Gar* is emphatic in John 9: 30, "This is *indeed* marvelous"; I Corinthians 11: 22, where the force of "What?" (King James) and "What!" (Moffatt, Montgomery, Revised Standard) might be rendered "The very idea!" In 15: 9, *gar* might be interpreted as illative, or as explanatory, but it also fits the context if given an emphatic rendering, *"Indeed* [or actually] I am [double nominative] the least of the apostles." In Acts 16: 37, emphatic *gar* shows the strong force of Paul's statement, "And now do they thrust us out secretly? *Never!"* (No indeed! or Not at all!). Goodspeed says, "By no means!" In 4: 16 *gar* is translated *indeed* by King James, American Standard, English Revised, Godbey, and others. Moffatt says, "a miracle has *admittedly* been worked by them."

Emphatic *gar* is used with the optative mode (the mode used to express a wish or to express hesitant affirmation) in Acts 8: 31 to indicate the inadequacy the Ethiopian felt about understanding the Scriptures. When asked by Philip if he really understood what he was reading, he replied, "How *indeed* can I unless someone shall guide me?" The emphatic force of *gar* here is reflected by, "Why, how can I?" (Moffatt, Goodspeed, Montgomery, Weymouth, Confraternity), and by "How in the world could I?" (Williams).

Gar seems to be emphatic in Romans 2: 28, *"Actually* (in fact) he is not a Jew who has the outward marks . . . but the true Jew is one inwardly." Paul is very fond of emphatic *gar.* Compare Romans 2: 14; 7: 15; 8: 19; 9: 3, where it could be rendered *actually;* and 2: 12, 24; 4: 15; 5: 6; 6: 7; 7: 19; 8: 24; 9: 6; 10: 2, 16, where *indeed* is the idea. Note 5: 13, *"Certainly* sin was in the world prior to the Law." Also 4: 9b which could be translated, *"Emphatically* we reiterate, Abraham's faith was counted to him as righteousness."

Kai

The most frequent conjunction in the New Testament is *kai.* It occurs many times on every page. Of course it is used often as a copula or connective, but it has diversified uses. To try to see in *kai* always the same meaning is often to miss its force.

We are certain of five general classifications[3] for *kai:*

1. Transitional or continuative. The use of *kai* as a mere connective, *and.* This is its most common use, and examples are multitudinous.

2. Adjunctive, meaning *also.* There are numerous examples as in the following where *kai* is translated *also:* "I *also* am a man under authority" (Matt. 8:9); "Last of all the woman died *also"* (Mark 12:22); "Likewise *also* said they all" (14:31); *"also* the chief priests mocking" (15:31); "There were *also* women looking on" (15:40); "Go into Judea, that thy disciples *also* may see the works that thou doest" (John 7:3); "The chief priests consulted that they might put Lazarus *also* to death" (12:10).

Luke frequently uses *kai* in the adjunctive sense: "Therefore *also* that holy thing which shall be born of thee shall be called the Son of God" (Luke 1:35); "Thy cousin Elizabeth, she hath *also* conceived a son" (1:36); "We *also* forgive every one that is indebted to us" (11:4); "As it was in the days of Noah, so shall it be *also* in the days of the Son of man" (17:26). Note also Luke 4:23; 6:29; 11:18, 30, 34, 45; 12:8; 14:12, 26; 16:10; 19:19; 20:12, 31, 32; 22:20, 39, 59; 23:7, 32, 36, 38; 24:23.

3. Ascensive, meaning *even,* of which use of *kai* examples are plentiful: "With authority commandeth he *even* the unclean spirits, and they do obey him" (Mark 1:27); *"Even* the wind and the sea obey him" (4:41); "What wisdom is this which is given unto him, that *even* such mighty works are wrought by his hands?" (6:2); *"Even* the Son of man came not to be ministered unto, but to minister" (10:45); "All things whatsoever ye would that men should do to you, do ye *even* so to them" (Matt. 7:12); "shall be taken away *even* what he

[3]Following Dana and Mantey. For a treatment of all the conjunctions, see D-M, pp. 239-258.

has" (13:12); *"even* the King of Israel" (John 12:13, ASV, RSV). Compare Matthew 26:73; Luke 6:32-34; 7:49; 8:18, 25; 10:11, 17; 12:7; 16:21; 19:26; 20:37; Romans 8:23. And thus it is clear that the ascensive or climatic force of *kai* is a common idiom of Koine Greek.

4. Adversative, the idea of contrast or antithesis often expressed by *yet* or *but*. Compare "Yes, Lord, *yet* the little dogs habitually eat from the crumbs which are falling from their masters' table" (Matt. 15:27); "They that are sown upon the rocky places, who, when they hear the word, immediately with joy receive it; *but* they do not have root in themselves" (Mark 4:16-17); He "entered into an house, and would have no man know it: *but* he could not be hid" (7:24); *"but* have not seen ... *but* have not heard" (Luke 10:24). *Yet* or *and yet* is sometimes an appropriate rendering of adversative *kai;* e.g., "Yet he promised that he would give it to him for a possession" (Acts 7:5); "Light has come into the world, *yet* men loved darkness rather than light" (John 3:19); "Did not Moses give you the law *and yet* none of you keepeth the law?" (7:19). See the same expression for *kai* in John 16:32; 20:29 (KJV, ASV, Weymouth, and others). *However* or *nevertheless* would often express the force of adversative *kai;* e.g., *"Nevertheless* then I will declare to them, I never approved of you at all!" (Matt. 7:23); *"Nevertheless* wisdom is justified of all her children" (Luke 7:35).

5. Emphatic or intensive. This connotation for *kai* is unmistakable in a number of contexts; e.g., "The *very* hairs of your head are all numbered" (Matt. 10:30); "so as to deceive, if possible, the *very* elect" (24:24); "Many other signs *truly* did Jesus in the presence of his disciples" (John 20:30); "The Spirit searcheth all things, *yea,* the deep things of God" (I Cor. 2:10); *"indeed* bear with me" (II Cor. 11:1); "In the church I had rather speak five words with my understanding, that by my voice I might teach others *also"* (I Cor. 14:19). (The idea is that Paul might *actually* or *really* instruct others); "for verily when we were with you" (I Thess. 3:4). *In fact* is an accurate possibility for rendering the force of *kai* in Colossians 4:3; I Thessalonians 4:10, and other passages.[4]

---

[4]Cf. D-M, p. 251.

In addition to the general classifications of meanings for *kai*, it has a temporal force in Mark 15:25: "And it was the third hour *when* they crucified him." Renderings reflecting this connotation of *kai* include Moffatt, Goodspeed, Williams, Montgomery, Weymouth, Revised Standard, J. B. Phillips. Other passages in which *kai* has a temporal connotation include Luke 19:43; John 4:35; 7:33; Acts 5:7; and Hebrews 8:8.

In the light of the various possibilities for *kai*, the careful exegete will not be bound to any one translation for it, but will be guided by the contextual implications. Doctrines of far-reaching importance may hinge upon the proper rendering of a conjunction. John 3:5 is an example. Many theories have been set forth in the hope of explaining the statement of Jesus, *gennēthēi ex hudatos kai Pneumatos,* commonly rendered "born of water and the Spirit." (See *and* in this verse in King James, English Revised, American Standard, Moffatt, Godbey, Goodspeed, Montgomery, Weymouth, Revised Standard, J. B. Phillips, and others.)

One theory is that there is a textual problem in John 3:5, that Jesus did not utter the phrase *hudatos kai* (rendered "water and"), but that the expression is a gloss added later. We cannot accept the suggestion of a scribal accretion in this passage, because the manuscript evidence supports our reading.

The general interpretation sees two factors in the new birth—water and Spirit—and seeks an explanation which involves both. Some commentators hold that baptism is essential because it is the medium which the Spirit uses in effecting the spiritual birth. If that be true, why does Jesus mention water only once in his requirements (cf. vss. 3, 5, 7)?[5]

Another view is that two births are meant, one literal and one spiritual. "Some insist on the language in verse 6 as meaning the birth of the flesh coming in a sac of water in contrast to the birth of the Spirit."[6]

If water baptism is meant here, then it is an indispensable requisite for kingdom participation since Jesus is making general, universal statements. He says, "Unless a person [*tis,* anyone] is born anew he cannot enter the kingdom" (cf. vss. 3, 5); and in verse 7, "You [*humas,* plural pronoun, meaning *you*

[5]RWP, Vol. V, p. 45.
[6]*Ibid.,* p. 46.

persons, i.e., all of you] must be born anew." What Jesus sets forth here are timeless, changeless principles without any exceptions. On other occasions He saved people on the ground of their faith in him, apart from any demand for water baptism. Therefore, either John 3:5 is not a reference to water baptism, or Jesus is inconsistent. We cannot believe that the Son of God is inconsistent. Any seeming contradiction arises from misunderstanding of his words.

The solution to the problem is found in the significance of the conjunction *kai.* Earlier in this chapter, it was shown that a common idiom in Koine Greek is the ascensive use of *kai,* meaning *even.* This use best fits the context in John 3:5. Interpreting this conjunction ascensively the verse is translated: "Jesus answered, Verily, verily, I say to thee, Unless a person is born of water, *even* of the Spirit, he cannot enter into the kingdom of God." This interpretation stands upon solid linguistic grounds and is in harmony with the immediate context, with the Johannine use of water as a symbol of the Holy Spirit, and with the general tenor of the Scriptures.

In the immediate context the emphasis of Jesus is upon spiritual experience and not upon any form or ritual. Water is mentioned only once (as a symbol of the Spirit), whereas the Spirit is mentioned expressly three times, and a fourth time by implication in the allusion to birth, *anōthen, from above* or *anew.* The belief current among the Jews in those days was that they were God's children and were in his kingdom by virtue of their natural birth as descendants of Abraham. Jesus refuted that false conception and taught that a spiritual transformation wrought by the Spirit of God is the only means of entrance into the Kingdom. (Cf. the emphasis of the Baptist, Matt. 3:7-12.)

The Johannine interpretation of water as a symbol for the Spirit of God is unmistakable. John records Jesus' words to the woman of Samaria: "But whosoever drinketh of the water that I shall give him shall never thirst; but the water that I shall give him shall be in him a well of water springing up into everlasting life" (John 4:14). In 7:37-38 where Jesus extends the invitation to the thirsty to come to him and drink, and says that from within the believer shall flow rivers of living water, the Apostle then adds the interpretation: "But this spake he of the Spirit, which they that believe on him should receive" (vs. 39). Ignatius of Antioch, early in the second century, in the quotation to which we referred in our discussion of the use of *erōs* (see Chapter IV), used water as a figure of speech for the Spirit of God.

Robertson takes "water" in John 3:5 as a symbol signifying the Spirit. Dods says, "Water is not an actual spiritual agency in the second birth; it is only a symbol."[7] Adam Clarke wrote: "The water . . . was only an emblem of the Holy Spirit. . . . It is not necessary that by water and the Spirit in this place we should understand two different things: it is probably an elliptical form of speech for the Holy Spirit under the similitude of water."[8]

Note also the ascensive use of *kai* in Matthew 3:11 and Luke 3:16, "He shall baptize you with the Holy Spirit, *even* with fire."

[7]Marcus Dods, EGT, Vol. I, p. 713.
[8]*Clarke's Commentary*, p. 318.

CHAPTER X

Particles

The term particle is used with varying applications by Greek grammarians. Some scholars take it in a broad sense to include adverbs, prepositions, conjunctions, and interjections. Classification is arbitrary in the nature of the case, since the field is vast, and it is hardly possible to cover all the ground without overlapping. For the sake of simplicity we are using the term in this chapter in a restricted sense to designate the intensive or emphatic particles and the negative particles.

The Greeks expressed precise shades of thought and emotion by particles. They belong to the development of the sentence from simple to complex structure. "Particles mark the history of the effort to relate words with each other, clause with clause, sentence with sentence, paragraph with paragraph."[1] They have to do with the delicate implications of expression which are often difficult, if not impossible, to translate. In modern languages such distinction and emphasis depend upon the tone of voice and the manner of a speaker.

Robertson says emphatic particles were used more frequently in poetry, especially tragic poetry, than in other kinds of writing. He quotes Farrar in noting that in Homer these particles "sustain and articulate the pulses of emotion," and that "by them alone we can perceive that Greek was the language of a witty, refined, intellectual, sensitive and passionate people."[2]

Although the New Testament and the papyri do not use particles with the frequency of classical Greek, we find in the New Testament a plentiful and diversified use of them. By learning to understand and appreciate the significance of this fascinating category of syntax, the interpreter apprehends more

[1]R, p. 1144.
[2]R, p. 1145.

fully the precise thought of many Greek expressions. Of course all that is involved in spoken language cannot be carried over into writing. "Indeed, it is not possible to put into mere written language all that the look, and gesture, the tone of voice, the emphasis of the accent carried when heard and seen."[3] How wonderful must have been the magnetism of the actual speech of Jesus and Paul for those individuals who saw and heard!

Intensive Particles

The intensive or emphatic particles express various shades of thought or emotion by emphasizing a particular word or by placing stress upon an entire sentence. The translator has the problem of deciding which word or phrase best brings out the force of a particle. The context is always the basic factor in determining the most adequate translation.

There are many illustrations of how the particles flash gleams of truth before the mind of the student of the Greek New Testament. Paul uses *ge* to intensify his statement in Romans 8:32, "He that [then follows *ge,* meaning *indeed, actually, even, went so far as, did as much as this*] spared not his own Son, but delivered him up for us all, how shall he not with him also freely give us all things?" This emphasizes the limitless love and grace of God. The fact that he has given the supreme gift implies that he will give everything else we need. The less is included in the greater. "The Christian's faith in providence in an inference from redemption."[4]

Note the strong inferential force of *dē* with the aorist imperative denoting urgency in I Corinthians 6:20, "For you were bought with a price: *now* [or *indeed, really, by all means* therefore] glorify God in your body." Findlay points out that the command to glorify God *in,* not *with,* the body, makes it the temple wherein each man serves as priest.[5] "Paul's argument stands four-square for the dignity of the body as the sanctuary of the Holy Spirit united to the Lord Jesus."[6]

The most common intensive particle in the New Testament is *men.* Its original function was "emphatic confirmation of single words, usually the weightiest word in the sentence."[7]

3 *Loc. cit.*
4 James Denney, EGT, Vol. II, p. 652.
5 G. G. Findlay, EGT, Vol. II, p. 822.
6 RWP, Vol. IV, p. 123.
7 R, p. 1151.

It may be translated *surely, indeed, in truth,* and the like. Sometimes *men* has a concessive force (e.g., II Cor. 11:4, "For if *indeed* he that comes proclaims another Jesus"), and there are instances where it implies contrast. "Its most common usage is to help differentiate the word or clause with which it occurs from that which follows."[8] Note its antithetical force with the conjunction *de* as an adversative particle in Matthew 3:11 and Luke 3:16, "I *indeed* baptize you with water . . . but . . . he shall baptize you with the Holy Spirit, even with fire." See this same idiom in Matthew 20:23 "You shall *indeed* [*men*] drink of my cup, *but* [*de*] to sit on my right and on my left is not mine to give." Note one of the most solemn of all antitheses in Jesus' vivid picture of the judgment when the ultimate moral separation of the human race takes place, the sheep *indeed* (*men*) being placed in a position of glory, *but* (*de*) the goats receiving their doom (25:33). It was common in Palestine to see a shepherd separating the sheep from the goats. Robertson refers to a shepherd standing at the gate and tapping the sheep to go to the right and the goats to the left.[9] In Acts 3:13, *men* along with the emphatic use of the personal pronoun *humeis* intensifies Peter's statement: "Jesus, whom *you yourselves indeed* [or, *you indeed on your part*] delivered up and denied." Luke uses *men* with the conjunction *oun* to introduce a parenthetical explanation (Acts 1:18-19) of the tragic fate of Judas. For a detailed discussion of all the intensive particles, see D-M, pages 258-267; R, pages 1142-1177.

Negative Particles

There are two principal negative particles in Greek, *ou* and *mē*. Their function in the New Testament is much the same as it was in the earlier Attic Greek. A careful observance of the force of the negative particles makes many passages of the New Testament more meaningful than is possible otherwise.

Ou is the stronger of the two negatives. It is positive, definite, and categorical, whereas *mē* is doubtful, indefinite, and hypothetical. Dana and Mantey call *ou* the particle of summary negation and *mē* the particle of qualified negation. Robertson says, "*Ou* denies the reality of an alleged fact. It is the clear-cut,

[8]D-M, p. 261.
[9]RWP, Vol. I, p. 201.

point-blank negative, objective, final."[10] He says *mē* is "a hesi-
tating negative, an indirect or subjective denial, an effort to
prevent (prohibit) what has not yet happened. It is the negative
of will, wish, doubt. If *ou* denies the fact, *mē* denies the idea."[11]
Inasmuch as *ou* is the stronger negative, its most frequent use
is with the indicative mode, but it is used also with the subjunctive and with the infinitive and the participle. *Mē*, which denies
hypothetically and hesitantly, is used most frequently with
the subjunctive and optative, modes which imply uncertainty.
"It also predominates with imperatives, infinitives, and participles, but it is used sparingly with the indicative."[12]

The most common use of *ou* is to make an assertion negative.
See "it did not fall" (Matt. 7:25); "they did not receive him"
(John 1:11); "I did not come to destroy" (Matt. 5:17).

Ou is frequent with the future indicative in prohibitions.
See "Thou shalt not tempt the Lord thy God" (Matt. 4:7);
"Man shall not live by bread alone" (Matt. 4:4); "Thou shalt
not commit murder" (Matt. 5:21).

Mē is used in negative hypothetical assertions. See John 3:18:
"The one who does not go on believing [in Him] is in a state
of condemnation [force of the perfect tense] already, because
he has not believed with abiding results [perfect tense] in the
name of the only Son of God."

Mē is used with the aorist subjunctive in prohibitions. See
Matthew 5:17: "Do not suppose [or do not begin to suppose,
ingressive emphasis of the aorist] that I came to destroy the
law or the prophets."

Mē is used with the present imperative in prohibitions. See
Matthew 7:1: "Stop judging [or Do not get the habit of judging, linear force of the present tense]; John 6:20: "Stop being
afraid!"

Intensive Compound Negatives

There are a number of compounds with *ou* and *mē* which
strengthen and intensify the negative idea. For example, the
neighbors and kinsmen of Zacharias and Elizabeth attempted
to call (*ekaloun*, conative imperfect, *were trying to call*) the

[10]R, p. 1156.
[11]R, p. 1167.
[12]D-M, pp. 264, 265.

child after the name of his father Zacharias, but Elizabeth said, *Ouchi,* "No!" (*Absolutely not!*). "But he shall be called John" (Luke 1:60). Compare Jesus' strong statement, "I tell you, *Nay*" (*Ouchi, Emphatically, no!*) (13:3); "No *man* [*oudeis*] can serve two masters" (Matt. 6:24); "*Never at any time* [*oudepote*] did I approve of you" (7:23); "*Not even* [*oude*] Solomon in all his glory was clothed like one of these" (6:29). Compare Mark 12:24, "Not knowing the scriptures, neither [*mēde, not even*] the power of God"; "Ever learning and *never* [*mēdepote*] able to come to the knowledge of the truth" (II Tim. 3:7). Note James 1:13, "Let *no man* [*mēdeis*] say when he is tempted, I am tempted of God: for God cannot be tempted with evil, neither tempteth he *any man*" (literally, *no one, oudena*).

Sometimes a series of negative words is used to strengthen a previous negative. "Not even with a chain was any one longer able to bind him" (Mark 5:3). Literally this verse reads, "Not even [*oude*] with a chain no longer [*ouketi*] no one [*oudeis*] was able to bind him"; "Where never any one had yet lain" (literally, "Where never no one had not yet lain") (Luke 23:53); "Owe no man anything" (literally, "Owe nothing to no one") (Rom. 13:8); "Apart from me you can do nothing" (literally, "Apart from me you are not able to do nothing") (John 15:5).

There are times when the two negatives are used together for powerful emphasis. "Him that cometh to me I will *in no wise* [*ou mē*] cast out" (John 6:37); "Lord, this shall *in no wise* [*ou mē*] be to Thee" (Matt. 16:22); "Nothing shall *by any means* [*ou mē*] hurt you" (Luke 10:19). Twice we have *ou mē* in Hebrews 13:5, "I will *in no wise* leave thee, nor will I *in any wise* forsake thee." Note Jesus' use of the double negative for strong emphasis in his prediction, "There shall *in no wise* [*ou mē*] be left here stone upon stone which shall not be thrown down" (Matt. 24:2). How must the listeners have felt who heard that prophecy of the utter destruction of their temple buildings and courts? Jesus' words, marking the tragic fall of Jerusalem, were fulfilled when the Roman armies under Titus destroyed the city in A.D. 70.

Ou and Mē with Questions

Here we have another most interesting idiom. When the negative particles are used in interrogative sentences, they indicate the kind of answer anticipated. Where the indicative mode is used, a question introduced by *ou* implies that an affirmative answer is expected, and a question introduced by *mē* implies that a negative answer is expected.

There are many examples of the use of *ou* in questions which expect the answer "Yes." Compare Mark 4:38, "Teacher, it is a care to thee, isn't it, that we are perishing?" The disciples felt in their hearts that Jesus really cared and that he would rescue them. In Matthew 13:55 f., *ou* is used three times in introducing the derogatory questions of Jesus' countrymen who were insinuating that he was only an ordinary carpenter. They could not understand how one of their fellow citizens of Nazareth could possess the wisdom Jesus demonstrated in his teaching. In Matthew 7:22, *ou*, while not repeated with each verb, is the negative of a series of questions, each expecting an affirmative answer; however, Jesus' reply reveals the startling fact that there will be judgment-day surprises for many people. For other examples where *ou* anticipates an affirmative answer, see Matthew 18:33; Mark 8:17 f.; Luke 17:17 f.; John 7:19; 9:8; Acts 9:21; I Corinthians 9:1.

Examples are plentiful of the use of *mē* in questions which expect the answer "No." "If his son shall ask bread, he will not give him a stone, will he? Or if he shall ask a fish, he will not give him a serpent, will he?" (Matt. 7:9 f.). Jesus says this illustrates God's readiness to give good things to those who keep on asking (present tense) him (vs. 11). In Luke 11:13, Jesus names the Holy Spirit as the supreme good. Note the force of *mē* in 22:35, "When I sent you . . . you didn't lack anything, did you? And they said, *Nothing whatsoever*" (*outhenos*). As one reads John 6:67, he can almost hear the pathos in the voice of Jesus as he asks the faithful group of disciples, "You also do not wish to go away, do you?" Jesus indicates his faith in them by his use of *mē* which expects a negative answer. He gets it from Simon Peter, whose reply has echoed across the centuries, "Lord, to whom shall we go? thou hast the words of eternal life" (vs. 68). Note also Jesus' pointed but polite question in John 21:5, which might be rendered, "Fellows, you aren't catching any fish, are you?" He gives them directions, and they make a great catch. It is a miracle similar to the one recorded in Luke 5:4 ff.

In I Corinthians 12:29-30, *mē* introduces every question, which indicates that Paul expects a negative answer each time: "Are all apostles? etc." We might translate the passage: "All are not apostles, are they? All are not prophets, are they? All are not teachers, are they? All do not perform works of power, do they? All do not have gifts of healings, do they? All do not speak with tongues, do they? All are not interpreters, are they?"

For other passages where *mē* introduces a question which expects the answer "No," see Romans 11:1; I Corinthians 1:13; John 4:33; 7:31, 47 f., 51 f.

Compound Negatives in Questions

The negative particles are used in various compounds to introduce questions. In such constructions they expect the same answers as when used simply, but have more emphatic force. For instance, in Matthew 13:55, *ou* is used twice, but *ouchi* intensifies the idea in verse 56: "*Certainly* all his sisters are with us, aren't they?" In 12:11, Jesus uses the stronger form *ouchi* to introduce his question regarding a man who rescues a sheep on the Sabbath: "Certainly he will lay hold of it and lift it up, will he not?" The application of the truth is obvious: A man is of infinite worth, hence it is lawful to act for his well-being, even on the Sabbath. *Ouchi* in Luke 24:32 means, "Our heart was really burning within us, wasn't it, as he was speaking to us in the way, as he was opening to us the Scriptures?" In I Corinthians 9:1, Paul introduces the first two questions with *ouk*[13], the third with *ouchi,* and the fourth with *ou.* Compare *ouchi,* anticipating strong negative answers, in Matthew 18:12; John 11:9; Romans 8:32.

As with *ou,* there are numerous illustrations of intensifying compounds with *mē.* For example, *mēti* is very effective in John 4:29, "This man is not the Christ, is he?" The Samaritan woman has the conviction that Jesus is the Messiah, but frames her question in a doubtful manner so as not to antagonize the

---

[13]*Ou* is spelled *ouk* before words beginning with vowels with smooth breathing, and *ouch* before those with vowels having rough breathing.

townsmen. By using *mēti* which only dimly conceals her attitude, "she raises the question and throws a cloud of uncertainty and curiosity over it with a woman's keen instinct."[14] She is challenging the thinking of the group.

When Jesus announced to the apostles that one of them would betray Him, they were exceedingly grieved. After some moments of startled silence, the eleven in quick succession asked, "It isn't I, is it, Lord?" (Matt. 26:22, *mēti* with the double nominative *egō eimi*, "Surely I am not the one, am I, Lord?"). Judas tries to assume a pose of innocence. He puts on a bold front with his question which expects a negative answer, "Surely I am not the one, am I, Rabbi?" (vs. 25). Judas uses the same terminology as the eleven had used, except they addressed Jesus, *Kurie* (Lord), whereas Judas says, *Rabbi,* probably an unintentional betrayal of his true estimate of Jesus. The Lord's reply, "You have said," means "Yes." (Compare John 18:37 for another example of this Jewish method of affirmation by using the statement of a questioner.)

Jesus did all he could to influence Judas to change his plans, repent, and be redeemed. Our Lord even washed the feet of the twelve, including Judas. But man is a free moral agent, and Judas made his decision by his own volition. John's dramatic statement that Judas went out "and it was night" (13:30) has both a literal and a spiritual application. Judas went forth into the night of ultimate tragedy, the night of hopelessness and despair, the night of remorse and grief, the night of eternal doom. Thus it is for every person who departs from Jesus the Light of the world.

For other questions introduced by *mēti,* see Matthew 7:16; 12:23; John 18:35; II Corinthians 1:17.

Perhaps a word should be said about the distinction made between negativing a word and negativing a sentence. There are examples in which *mē* is the interrogative particle introducing a sentence, while *ou* blends with the verb. In Romans 10:18, *mē* expects a negative answer to the question, while *ou* negates the verb: "They did not fail to hear, did they?" See the same idiom in verse 19 and I Corinthians 9:4 f. Note also 11:22: "The very idea!" (emphatic force of the conjunction *gar*). "You do not fail to have houses in which to eat and drink, do you?"

---

[14] R, p. 1167.

CHAPTER XI

Cases

Our word "case," Old French *cas*, Latin *casus*, from *cadere* (to fall, happen), represents the Greek *ptōsis* which means "falling." The substantive is regarded as "falling" in a certain relationship to the other parts of the sentence. The nominative case is considered as falling in a perpendicular or direct relation to the rest of the sentence; the other cases as falling in an oblique or indirect relation. Thus the term oblique may be applied to any case except the nominative and the vocative.[1]

Cases have to do with the changes of form (inflection) of a noun, pronoun, or adjective, that indicates its relation to other words as that of subject, object, instrument, and the like. In English this relation is generally expressed by prepositions and by the position of words in the sentence. In Greek, changes of form, like different word endings, mark such distinctions as case, gender, number, mode, tense, person, voice.

There are eight cases in New Testament Greek. This is evident from the results of comparative philology and from the nature of the case idea.

Studies in comparative grammar have convinced scholars that there were originally eight separate case forms as well as eight case ideas in the Indo-European family of languages.[2] The Sanskrit, which is the oldest member of the family and which retained many of the characteristics of the parent speech, reflects eight case forms. Robertson says, "The Anglo-Saxon preserved six distinct case forms and in some words all eight."[3]

The eight cases have had a varied history in all the Indo-European languages. Gradually there occurred a coalescing of the case forms until, in the Greek language, there were only

---

[1]The vocative is not a case in the strict sense, but it is treated as such by grammarians for the sake of a convenient classification.
[2]D-M, p. 65; R, p. 446.
[3]RSG, p. 86.

five different forms in the classical and in the Koine periods. The increasing use of prepositions was responsible for the diminishing or blending of the case forms. Earlier case endings served to express word relations. But, at best, the inflections could express relationship only in a general way. As language became more complex, the cases needed help to convey clearly the diverse ideas. Consequently there arose the use of adverbs with cases in order to make the meaning more accurate. "Even in the later Sanskrit a number of set case forms (adverbs) came to be used with some of the cases to make clearer the exact relations of words, whereas in the older Sanskrit no such helpers were felt to be needed."[4] Giles has noted that these adverbs, which are now called prepositions, in time became the constant concomitants of cases.

The diminishing of the case endings, apparent in Greek and Latin, has reached its climax in modern English and French. In present-day English, with the exception of the personal pronouns, the six Anglo-Saxon case endings have all disappeared but one, the genitive "s," and it is sometimes represented by the apostrophe or displaced by the preposition "of." The modern Greek vernacular has only three case forms: nominative, genitive, and accusative.

The second forceful argument for eight cases in the Greek of the New Testament is the fact that case is basically a matter of function rather than of form. "The case of the Greek noun is to be determined by its relation to the rest of the sentence."[5] Each case has a distinctive idea, and it is function that calls forth the appropriate case. Hence, there are as many cases as there are functions of the noun.

Thus it is to be remembered that in New Testament Greek there are eight cases (because there are eight functions of a noun) appearing under five case forms. The genitive and ablative have the same inflectional endings, while the locative, dative, and instrumental have the same forms. In other words, the syncretism or blending of the case forms has not obliterated the case ideas. A genitive remains a genitive, and an ablative remains an ablative, although both came to have the same forms. The interpreter, if he is to gather the resultant idea in a given

[4]R, p. 450.
[5]D-M, p. 65.

instance, will study the meaning of a word, the primary significance of the particular case, the preposition (if one is used), and the context. Sometimes the blended cases may be translated as either one or the other with equal correctness, like the example in Acts 2:33 which may be rendered *exalted at* (locative), *exalted by* (instrumental), or *exalted to* (dative) "the right hand of God." Compare the same possibilities in Romans 8:24 where Paul says we are saved *in hope, by hope,* or *for hope.*

The noun is cast in many roles in syntax. Its various functions and relations involve the cases. A brief discussion of each case should be helpful to the general reader.

Nominative

The most frequent and typical role of the noun is its use as the subject of a sentence. As such it is said to be in the nominative case which corresponds to the English nominative. Early in the history of the language, the subject of the sentence was indicated by the personal endings of the verb. But a verb ending was often indefinite (no distinction between he, she, it), hence, a noun was frequently used to express the subject more exactly. Finally the noun came to be regarded as the subject of the sentence, the noun subject being in apposition with the subject expressed by the verb itself.

So the nominative is the naming or designating case. As Dana and Mantey put it, "The nominative is more than the case of the subject: it is the case of specific *designation.*"[6]

There is an interesting idiom with the nominative in regard to case agreement. A word is sometimes retained in the nominative instead of being put in the case of the word with which it is in apposition. This variation is quite common in the Apocalypse of John. For example, in 1:5, *the faithful witness, the firstborn, the ruler,* are all in the nominative although in apposition with *Jesus Christ* (ablative). See also 2:13, where *my faithful martyr* (nominative) is in apposition with *Antipas* (genitive); 2:20, where *calleth* (nominative articular participle) is in apposition with *the woman* (accusative); 3:12, where *which cometh down* (nominative articular participle) is in apposition with *the new Jerusalem* (genitive); and 20:2,

---

[6]D-M, p. 69.

the old serpent (nominative) in apposition with *the dragon* (accusative). Robertson says such examples are in accord with the ancient Greek idiom. He gives illustrations from the papyri.[7]

In Revelation 1:4 we have the expressions *the one who is, and the one who was, and the one who is coming,* all in the nominative following the preposition *apo* (from) which ordinarily is used with the ablative case. This use of the nominative emphasizes the divine and changeless nature of God.[8] Compare the same force of the nominative in Revelation 1:8; 4:8; 11:17; 16:5. The expressions *the one who is, and who was, and who is coming* may be an amplification of the phrase *I am The Being,* or *I am He who is* (Exod. 3:14, Septuagint). The writer of the Revelation frequently adopts titles which the Greek translators used to express the character of the God of Israel, such as The Almighty (Rev. 1:8; 4:8; 11:17; 15:3; 16:7, 14; 19:6, 15; 21:22); The Holy and True (Rev. 3:7; 6:10); The First and the Last (Rev. 2:8).

Perhaps a word should be said concerning the critical view which has amplified unreasonably the solecisms (deviations from ordinary rules of grammar) found in the Revelation, and the differences of language and style between the Apocalypse and the other Johannine writings. There are, to be sure, linguistic differences between the Revelation and the Fourth Gospel and the Epistles of John. Does this mean that the same author did not write all these books? Not at all. Or may John be regarded as the author of Revelation only by contending that he wrote it early before he knew Greek well? To say that John was not able to handle Greek is untrue, for the Apocalypse contains much excellent Greek. Its writer gives abundant proof that he was well acquainted with the principles and even the finer points of Greek grammar.

So the grammatical irregularities of Revelation are not those of a linguistic novice, but are intentional and meaningful. Charles says, "We have found that these abnormalities are not instances of mere licence nor yet mere blunders, as they have been most wrongly described, but are constructions deliberately

---

[7]R, pp. 458, 414.
[8]Cf. RSG, p. 90; R, pp. 414, 459.

chosen by our author."[9] Concerning the nominatives after the
preposition *apo* in Revelation 1:4, Charles remarks, "The Seer
has deliberately violated the rules of grammar in order to preserve the divine name inviolate from the change which it
would necessarily have undergone if declined."[10]

Randell acknowledges that "many of our so-called solecisms
are capable of being brought under well-known usages, whereby even the best classical authors are held to be justified in
departing from ordinary grammatical laws." Randell also says,
regarding the character of the Greek of the Apocalypse, "Most,
if not all, of its peculiarities may be due to the Hebrew training
of the author of the book; and, on the other hand, many of them
have parallels in profane Greek literature."[11]

With respect to discord in case or gender in the Revelation
of John, Robertson shows that other books of the New Testament reflect such phenomena, including the writings of Luke
and Paul; that there are similar examples in the Septuagint;
"and indeed occasionally in the very best of Greek writers."
He says, "One must not be a slavish martinet in such matters
at the expense of vigour and directness."[12]

Lenski's answer to the question regarding the linguistic differences between the Revelation and the other Johannine
writings is that the Lord intended the language of the Apocalypse to be different for an obvious purpose: "This book is
in the highest sense Jesus Christ's book, and the very language
proclaims that great fact."[13]

Genitive

Mention has been made of the blending of case forms in the
history of the Indo-European languages, and of such syncretism
in the Greek of the New Testament. Now we come to consider
a case which shares its form with another. The genitive and
ablative have the same case ending, but they have different
functions. Comparative grammar has shown that historically
they are separate cases and express different ideas.

[9]R. H. Charles, *The Revelation of St. John* (*The International Critical Commen-*
tary), Vol. I, p. clii.
[10]*Ibid.*, p. 10.
[11]Rev. T. Randell, *The Revelation of St. John the Divine* (*The Pulpit Commen-*
tary), p. xxiii.
[12]R, p. 414 ff.
[13]R. C. H. Lenski, *The Interpretation of St. John's Revelation*, p. 15 f.

Inasmuch as the same form may represent either the genitive or the ablative, the first question an interpreter must solve when confronted with this form is which case it is. Although there are examples that can be taken either as genitive or as ablative, the context usually indicates one or the other. The chief use of the ablative in the New Testament is with verbs and prepositions. Therefore as a general rule it may be presumed that if the form is used with another noun, it is the genitive.

The root idea of the genitive is genus or kind, hence it is the specifying case. It defines or describes. Dana and Mantey observe that it "usually limits a substantive or substantival construction, though its use is not infrequent with verbs, adjectives, and adverbs. Its adjectival nature is very pronounced and quite obvious."[14] In its function of definition and limitation, the genitive brings the implications of an idea into a definite scope, specifically with reference to class or kind. The genitive case limits as to kind, whereas the accusative case limits as to extent.

The principal use of the genitive is with substantives. A genitive with another noun describes it in some respect. Because something may be pictured from a number of viewpoints, the genitive may have a variety of meanings. It may describe from such standpoints as ownership (genitive of possession, "servant of the high priest," Matt. 26: 51); relationship ("James the son of Zebedee," 4: 21); value (genitive of price, "a measure of wheat for a denarius," Rev. 6: 6); quality ("the body of sin," Rom. 6: 6); and others.

A noun in the genitive may stand in apposition to another noun in order to further define it. For example, Paul places his own name in apposition with "a servant of Christ Jesus" (Rom. 1: 1). In II Corinthians 1: 22 and 5: 5, "the *earnest* [*arrabōn*, seal, pledge, foretaste] of the Spirit" means the Holy Spirit is the pledge or down payment of salvation (cf. Eph. 1: 14). Note the appositional use of the genitive in II Corinthians 5: 1, where Paul calls our earthly house a tent-home. He uses this figure to contrast our present state with our future existence. According to the Apostle's metaphor, our earthly life is temporary,

---
[14]D-M, p. 72.

like living in a tent which may be taken down at any hour. But when the terrestrial abode is no more, we have the celestial existence awaiting us, and it is everlasting. Note other genitives of apposition or definition such as "crown of life" (Rev. 2:10), "crown of righteousness" (II Tim. 4:8), and "crown of glory" (I Pet. 5:4).

According to the genius of the case, all genitives are more or less descriptive, but there are examples in which the descriptive character is especially prominent. The expression "baptism of repentance" (Mark 1:4; Luke 3:3; Acts 13:24; 19:4) has already been mentioned in Chapter VII.

When the genitive is used with nouns of action, it may be either subjective or objective. If the noun in the genitive produces the action, it is called the subjective genitive. If the noun in the genitive receives the action, it is called the objective genitive. Sometimes it is difficult to tell whether a genitive is the subject or the object of the verbal idea. It is a matter for the context and general usage to decide. For example, "the love of Christ constraineth us" (II Cor. 5:14) could mean the love we have for Christ (objective genitive) or the love Christ has for us (subjective genitive). The immediate context does not indicate which it is, but the wider context of New Testament usage implies that Paul means Christ's love for him is the motivating influence of his life (cf. Rom. 8:39; Gal. 2:20).

Notice the subjective genitive in these passages from Romans: "the obedience which faith produces" (1:5); "righteousness which springs from faith" (4:13 and compare 10:6); "God's love for us has been poured forth into and continues to inundate [perfect tense of verb] our hearts through the Holy Spirit who has been given to us" (5:5).

Also we find frequent examples of the objective genitive; e.g., "the blasphemy against the Holy Spirit" (Matt. 12:31); "the testimony concerning Jesus Christ" (I Cor. 1:6); "the love for the truth" (II Thess. 2:10).

In a sense both the objective and subjective ideas are seen in a passage like Romans 8:35, "Who shall separate us from the love of Christ?" (the love we have for him, and the love he has for us).

Ablative

From the Latin term *ablativus,* meaning that which is carried away or separated, we have the fundamental significance of the ablative case. It indicates origin, derivation, or source. Dana and Mantey say, "Its basal significance is point of departure. . . . Hence, in simplest terms we may say its root idea is separation."[15]

We have seen that the genitive is the specifying case. The ablative is the "whence case," as it is commonly termed by grammarians. The genitive describes, while the ablative denotes separation. In ascertaining the specific idea of the genitive-ablative form, it is helpful to ask whether a given instance indicates kind (genitive) or source (ablative).

In the New Testament the ablative is used infrequently with adjectives, but it is common with adverbs and prepositions. With verbs the ablative is not used as often as the accusative, genitive, or dative, but it occurs rather often where the idea of origin or separation is dominant.[16] Verbs which contain a comparative or partitive idea naturally take the ablative, as comparison implies separation in degree.[17]

When used with verbs expressing a partitive idea, there is a contrast between the genitive-ablative, either of which accents a part, and the accusative which signifies the whole. For example, note both these ideas in Revelation 2:17: "I will give to him *of the hidden manna* [ablative, or partitive genitive, *some of the manna*], and I will give to him *a white pebble*" (accusative, meaning the whole). Compare *"things sacrificed to idols"* (accusative) in verse 14, and "Let him eat *of the bread,* and let him drink *of the cup*" (ablatives) (I Cor. 11:28). Compare Matthew 15:27, "The little dogs have the habit of eating [present tense of linear action] *some of the small morsels*" (preposition *apo* with the ablative). Note also the partitive idea in Matthew 26:27, regarding the cup. Jesus says, *"All of you [pantes,* masculine plural] drink *some of it"* (preposition *ek* with the ablative singular pronoun agreeing with *cup*). So the "all" does not refer to the contents of the cup, but to the disciples. Jesus com-

---

[15]D-M, p. 81.
[16]RSG, p. 104 ff.
[17]D-M, p. 82.

mands all of them to drink from the cup, and Mark 14:23 says, "and they all drank *of it*" (ablative).

When a noun in the ablative case is used to modify another substantive, the idea of origin, separation, or source is prominent. Thus the expression *ekklēsiai tou theou* (church of God), found eleven times in the New Testament,[18] emphasizes the origin of the church. The church is a divinely established institution. Jesus Christ is its founder and builder (Matt. 16:18). He is the sovereign ruler and head (Eph. 1:22), and salvation is the basis of membership for all people (Acts 2:47).

The phrase *ekklēsiai tou theou* can also be interpreted as the possessive genitive case, denoting the ownership of the church. It belongs to God, not to any group or faction (cf. I Cor. 1:2 ff.). In verse 2 the perfect passive participle "sanctified" is in apposition with "church of God," defining the church as consisting of persons who are in the state of having been sanctified in Christ Jesus. (Sanctification is here used broadly to signify all the aspects of salvation involved in the Christian experience.)

Of the 114 occurrences of the term *ekklēsia* (assembly, church) in the New Testament, the great majority of them refer to the local congregation. Dana and Sipes assign a total of 93 occurrences or 81 per cent to the local sense.[19]

Locative

As already mentioned, the locative, instrumental, and dative cases are all expressed in the Greek of the New Testament by the same inflectional form, but each maintains its distinctive idea. Possibly the different forms for these three cases survived until a comparatively late period in the history of the language. According to Brugmann, the locative and instrumental forms coalesced, and afterwards the dative blended its case ending with theirs.[20]

When the exegete is confronted with a locative-instrumental-dative form, he will remember that one of three basic ideas is expressed thereby: place (locative), means (instrumental), or personal interest (dative). Generally it is not as difficult to grasp the distinction as might be presumed, although in some

---

[18]Acts 20:28; I Cor. 1:2; 10:32; 11:16, 22; 15:9; II Cor. 1:1; Gal. 1:13; I Thess. 2:14; II Thess. 1:4; I Tim. 3:5.
[19]H. E. Dana and L. M. Sipes, *A Manual of Ecclesiology*, p. 67.
[20]RSG, p. 111.

instances it is hardly possible to decide whether the form is locative, instrumental, or dative, e.g., whether in Acts 2:33 it is *at, by,* or *to* the right hand of God.

The name "locative," from the Latin *locus,* meaning "place," indicates the idea of this case. When a noun serves to indicate the position of an object or action, the locative case is used. It is the place case and answers the question, Where? "In Sanskrit Whitney calls it the *in* case, and so it is in Greek. It indicates a point within limits and corresponds in idea with the English *in, on, among, at, by,* the resultant conception varying according to the meaning of the words and the context." [21] "In simplest terms we may define the locative as the case of position." [22]

The locative is used with a spatial connotation, expressing location in space; e.g., "in the boat" (Mark 4:36); "in the stern" (vs. 38); "in a boat" (or instrumental "by ship" as King James) (Matt. 14:13); "in that road" (Luke 10:31); "in another way" (or instrumental, *by means of* another way) (Jas. 2:25). Note "in the Jordan river" (Matt. 3:6), where we have the preposition *en* (in) with the locative, stating where the baptizing took place. John baptized the people in the stream of Jordan. The etymology of the term *baptize* (which is a transliteration, not a translation), the spiritual truth it symbolizes (death, burial, resurrection of the believer into newness of life), and the setting in which it was administered, all imply that John practiced immersion. Compare Romans 6:3-5; Colossians 2:12.

The locative is used with a figurative connotation, expressing the sphere in which an action takes place. Compare the metaphorical expression "the poor in spirit" (Matt. 5:5) where Jesus says the realization of the kingdom of heaven comes to those who realize their spiritual poverty or need. In verse 8 Jesus shows the need for purity in the sphere of the heart as over against the outward ceremonies of mere ritualism.

The locative is used with a temporal connotation to express the time in which an action takes place; e.g., "in this night" (Mark 14:30); "Now on the last day" (John 7:37); "in the

[21]RSG, p. 106.
[22]D-M, p. 87.

resurrection at the last day" (11:24); "Now on the first (day) of the week (20:1).

Instrumental

The instrumental is the case of means or association, expressed in English by the prepositions *with, by,* and the like. It designates the instrument by which an action is accomplished.

This case is also called the associative-instrumental. It was probably preceded by the old associative case, of which traces are reflected in Sanskrit. Robertson thinks the associative was the earlier usage out of which the instrumental idea was logically developed. He observes that "most of the difference is due to the distinction between persons (association, accompaniment) and things (means, implement, instrument). . . . We have a similar combination in our English 'with' which is used in both senses."[23]

The instrumental case with the idea of association or accompaniment may be easily illustrated: "They followed him" (Mark 1:18); "he joined himself to a citizen of that country" (Luke 15:15); "he was conversing with him" (Acts 24:26). Note Paul's exhortation with the present imperative, "Stop getting heterogeneously yoked up with unbelievers" (II Cor. 6:14).

The instrumental is used to express the method or manner of an action. "If I partake with thanks" (I Cor. 10:30); "with her head uncovered" (11:5); "whether in pretense or in truth" (Phil. 1:18, RSV).

The instrumental case may denote the cause or occasion of an act; e.g., "I am perishing because of famine" (Luke 15:17); "because of unbelief they were broken off" (Rom. 11:20); "because of the cross of Christ" (Gal. 6:12).

The instrumental is used in temporal expressions where a considerable period of time is indicated. Thus "about the space of four hundred and fifty years" (Acts 13:20); "for a long time he had amazed them" (8:11); "for a long time" (Luke 8:27, 29); *Chronois aiōniois* (during time-ages) (Rom. 16:25) might be regarded as the means by which God's purpose is accomplished, or the associative idea might be prominent, "along with times eternal."[24]

---

[23]R, p. 526.
[24]RWP, Vol. IV, p. 430.

The most common usage of the instrumental case is to express means. Compare "bound with fetters and chains" (Mark 5:4); the disciples rubbing grain with their hands (Luke 6:1); "killed James the brother of John with the sword" (Acts 12:2); "by grace are ye saved" (Eph. 2:8); "Barnabas was carried away [strong double compound verb] by their hypocrisy" (Gal. 2:13). Note three examples of the instrumental of means in Luke 7:38: "with tears," "with her hair," and "with the ointment."

The significance of the instrumental sometimes approaches very closely that of the locative. In Judges 16:8 (Septuagint), we read that Samson was bound with cords, in such a way that he was *en autais* (in them)—he was located in the cords. The preposition *en* (in) with the instrumental of means is found also in verse 7, *with* seven moist cords; verse 11, *with* new ropes; verse 12, bound him *with* them (new ropes); verse 13, *"by what means* thou mayest be bound"; verse 14, *with* the web. Note also the instrumental case of means without the preposition in verse 13, "fasten them *with* the pin"; and verse 14, same idiom. In Matthew 3:11, where the preposition *en* (in) is used with reference to both water baptism and the baptism of the Holy Spirit, the construction might be interpreted either as the instrumental of means or as the locative of sphere. We have *en* with the instrumental case in Revelation 1:5: "The One who loves us, and has loosed us from our sins *by his blood";* and in 5:9: "Because thou wast slain and didst purchase for God *by thy blood* some of every tribe and tongue and people and nation."

Dative

The term dative is derived from the Latin *dativus,* based on the verb *dare,* to give. So the dative might be called the giving case. Its primary idea is personal interest or reference. It is used mainly with persons, although it is sometimes used of things, but of things personified. Robertson says, "The accusative, genitive, and dative are all cases of inner relations, but the dative has a distinctive personal touch not true of the others."[25] Dana and Mantey say of the dative: "It is primarily a case of personal relations, and it is with this in view that we must in-

[25]R, p. 536.

terpret it when applied to things. . . . The idea of interest as applied to things becomes *reference*."[26] Like the other cases, the dative has a variety of applications for its basic idea.

The most extensive and probably the earliest use of the dative is to indicate the indirect object of a verb. This function corresponds to our English *to* or *for*. Note, "I have something to say to you" (Luke 7:40, RSV); "yield to him also the cloak" (Matt. 5:40); "the things I write to you" (Gal. 1:20); "I will give to him the morning star" (Rev. 2:28).

The dative may be also the direct object of verbs which emphasize close personal relation like trust, distrust, envy, please, serve, and the like.

The dative may denote possession. This idiom is "personal interest particularized to the point of ownership,"[27] e.g., "to any man a hundred sheep" (Matt. 18:12); "the promise is to you" (Acts 2:39); "there was not for them a place" (Luke 2:7).

The dative may be used when the idea of reference is more prominent than the idea of interest. This dative of reference is applied mostly with things, but it may also be used with persons. Compare "We who died with reference to sin" (Rom. 6:2); "We are debtors, but not with reference to the flesh" (8:12); "Cease worrying with reference to your life, about what you might have to eat or drink; or with reference to your body, about what you might put on" (Matt. 6:25); "If we were out of our minds, it was with reference to God; if we are in our right minds, it is with reference to you" (II Cor. 5:13); "All the things written by the prophets with reference to the Son of man" (Luke 18:31).

The dative may be used where personal interest is affected favorably or unfavorably. In the former instance, it is called the dative of advantage; in the latter instance (the negative aspect of the same idiom), it is called the dative of disadvantage. Sometimes grammars call it the ethical dative. Examples of the dative of advantage include, "He made us a kingdom, priests for his God and Father" (Rev. 1:6); and "he made them a kingdom and priests for our God" (5:10); "It is expedient for you [it is to your advantage] that I go away" (John 16:7).

We have the dative of disadvantage in passages like these:

---

[26]D-M, p. 84.
[27]D-M, p. 85.

"You testify against yourselves" (Matt. 23:31); "We wipe off the dust against you" (Luke 10:11); "while crucifying [to their own destruction] the Son of God" (Heb. 6:6). A recognition of this idiom clarifies Paul's statement in I Corinthians 4:4 where he uses a reflexive pronoun in the dative case with the verb *sunoida* and a negative particle: "I know nothing against myself" (ASV). But Paul goes on to say that subjective approval does not mean that a person is right with God. The King James rendering: "For I know nothing by myself," is inaccurate. The sense of the passage is brought out by the American Standard, "For I know nothing against myself; yet am I not hereby justified: but he that judgeth me is the Lord." Others reflecting the proper connotation include Moffatt, Goodspeed, Weymouth, Williams, Montgomery, Revised Standard.

Accusative

The name "accusative" is not really accurate. It is from the Latin *accusativus,* used to translate a Greek term of which *cause* is the more likely idea. Robertson says the Old English "accuse" could mean "show," but calling it the showing case does not distinguish it from the other oblique cases. "Originally, however, it was the only case and thus did show the relations of nouns with other words."[28]

More important than the name is its history and function. The accusative is the oldest case of all, and probably the other oblique cases arose as variations or after developments from it. They were formed apparently in order to express more exactly the various word relations than was possible by the accusative.

It is difficult to ascertain the primary meaning of the accusative. "It must originally have had a great variety of uses, as a result of which its root idea is not easy to discern."[29] Delbruck did not think it was possible to find a single unifying idea, but only special types of the accusative. Various grammarians think of the accusative as "motion toward" the main idea, or the answer to the question, "How far?" or as the limitative case, or as the extension case, expanding the thought or the result of verbal action. Dana and Mantey prefer the term "limitation" in defining the basic function of the accusative

[28]RSG, p. 92; R, p. 466.
[29]D-M, p. 91.

whose root meaning, they say, involves three ideas: the direction, the extent, or the end of motion or action.[30]

Having arisen first in the history of the language, the accusative is naturally the most general in idea, and it has been the most widely used of all the cases.

The accusative is the case of the direct object, corresponding generally to the English direct object. The idea of extension or limitation is seen clearly when a noun receives the action expressed by a verb. Examples of the accusative of direct object are everywhere in the New Testament: "Behold I send my messenger" (Mark 1:2); "He saw Simon and Andrew his brother" (vs. 16); "They were bringing to him all those having it bad, and those demonized" (vs. 32).

The accusative may express extent as to time, and thus answers the question, How long? Compare, "Lo, these many years do I serve thee" (Luke 15:29); "He remained two days in the place where he was" (John 11:6); "They remained with him that day" (1:39). Goodspeed and Williams render John 1:39: "They spent the rest of the day with him." The same idea appears in Moffatt. When a person gets a vision of Jesus, nothing in the world has any more attraction. "To his latest day John never forgot the hour when first he met Jesus."[31] A point of time may be emphasized by the accusative (e.g., I Cor. 15:30; Rev. 3:3).

The accusative may express extent as to space, and thus answers the question, How far? "Having rowed about twenty-five or thirty stadia" (John 6:19); "having gone forward a little distance" (Matt. 26:39); "He withdrew from them about a stone's throw" (Luke 22:41, RSV).

When an accusative of the direct object has the same root as the verb, it is called a cognate accusative. Note such examples as, "They feared with great fear" (Mark 4:41); "sinning a sin" (I John 5:16); "I have fought the good fight" (II Tim. 4:7, RSV).

Vocative

The vocative (a noun used as the object of address) is justified in being called a case from the standpoint of function. But

---

[30] D-M, p. 92.
[31] RWP, Vol. V, p. 26.

the vocative is not an inherent part of the sentence, and it is without case endings. However, for syntactical purposes, it is treated as a case, although technically it is not. It stands alone and expresses a complete idea. Note how the words in the vocative, "Mary!" and "My Teacher!" "tell the whole story of recognition between Jesus and Mary" (John 20:16).[32]

The vocative has no inflectional form, but may resort to several expedients. Sometimes the simple vocative is used, e.g., "Theophilus" (Luke 1:3); "Father" (John 17:1); "Men of Athens" (Acts 17:22).

The inflectional particle O may be used with the vocative to give special force to address. "O man" (Rom. 2:1); "O Jews" (Acts 18:14). O with the vocative gives solemnity to a statement, as "O Theophilus" (1:1). In most of the New Testament examples, this idiom expresses emotion. Note "O woman, great is thy faith" (Matt. 15:28); "O faithless generation" (Mark 9:19). The tone may be that of censure or rebuke; e.g., "And you, O man, who are judging those who do such things, yet are practicing them yourself, do you suppose that you will escape God's judgment?" (Rom. 2:3); "Who are you, O man, to engage in controversy with God?" (9:20). Note the long expression in the vocative in Paul's denunciation of Elymas the sorcerer (Acts 13:10).

The article may be used with the vocative to ascribe special definiteness to the object of address. "Fear not, little flock" (or my little flock) (Luke 12:32); "Even so, Father [*ho Patēr*]" (Matt. 11:26); "Maid [*hē pais*], arise" (Luke 8:54). Note also the direct, positive command in Jesus' use of the article as he rebukes the dumb and deaf spirit in Mark 9:25. "Jesus addresses the demon as a separate being from the boy, as he often does. This makes it difficult to believe that Jesus was merely indulging popular belief in a superstition. He evidently regards the demon as the cause in this case of the boy's misfortune."[33] Thomas uses the article twice in his sublime exclamation, "My Lord and my God" (John 20:28). Thomas thus declares his assurance of Jesus' resurrection and his complete satisfaction regarding the deity of the Savior. For other

---

[32]R, p. 462; RWP, Vol. V, p. 312.
[33]RWP, Vol. I, p. 343.

examples of the article with the vocative where God is addressed, see Revelation 4:11; 6:10; 15:3.

Acts 9:7 Compared with Acts 22:9

A contradiction between Acts 9:7 and Acts 22:9 appears in a number of renderings, including King James, Moffatt, Godbey, Goodspeed, Williams, Confraternity, Revised Standard. An application of the significance of the Greek cases brings clarity to the expressions in question and shows that there is no contradiction in the Greek text.

According to Acts 9:7, the men who journeyed with Saul stood speechless, hearing the *voice* (*phōnēs,* genitive, the specifying case, telling what they heard). Acts 22:9 says they did not hear the *voice* (*phōnēn,* accusative, the case of extension, indicating the extent to which they heard). Actually they heard the voice, or sound, but did not hear to the extent that they understood. Also they saw the light (Acts 22:9), but did not see Jesus (9:7). Weymouth and Montgomery render Acts 9:7 in connection with 22:9, "hearing the voice . . . did not hear the words." The genitive with *akouō,* to hear, to understand, specifies the kind of sound; the accusative after this verb indicates the comprehension of the sound.

CHAPTER XII

The Article

The English word "article" goes back to the Latin *articulus* which has the same root as the Greek *arthron* (joint). The Greek grammarians called the article the limiting joint, which is more accurate, for one of the uses of the article is to limit the application of nouns.

Dana and Mantey have observed that nothing is more native to the Greek language than its use of the definite article.[1] Robertson refers to the article as a Greek contribution, a new departure among the Indo-European languages, and calls its development one of the most interesting things in human speech. "It is not essential to language, but certainly very convenient and useful. . . . Its free use leads to exactness and finesse."[2]

The article first appears in Homer and reaches its perfection in Attic prose, particularly in Plato whose works are rich in the use of the article. Robertson says the New Testament usage is in all essential respects in harmony with the Attic, more so than is true of the papyri. "The article has shown remarkable persistency and survives with very little modification in modern Greek."[3]

The Greek does not have an indefinite article. It was never developed in the history of the language. But there are some examples in the New Testament where the cardinal number *heis* (one), and the indefinite pronoun *tis* (someone, something, anything) are used with practically the same force as the English *a* or *an;* e.g., "And *a* scribe came to him" (Matt. 8:19); "And I saw, and heard *an* angel flying in midheaven" (Rev. 8:13); "And the sixth angel sounded his trumpet, and I heard

---

[1]D-M, p. 135.
[2]R, p. 754, 756.
[3]R, p. 754.

a voice from the four horns of the golden altar" (9: 13). In Luke 10: 25, *tis* has the force of an indefinite article. Same idiom appears in verse 30.

The nonuse of the article in Greek does not always mean that a noun is indefinite. The anarthrous substantive may be either definite or indefinite. That is to say, a word may be definite without the article, for there are several ways of making a thing definite. Certain words, like *scripture, sun, moon, sea, earth, heaven,* are so distinctive that they may be definite without the article. Proper names, because they already denote a definite individual, do not require the article. Terms like Lord, God, Jesus, Holy Spirit, are definite, although these expressions for Deity may also have the article. Anarthrous nouns may be made definite by the use of possessive pronouns, demonstrative pronouns, the genitive case, and by the use of prepositions.

Function of the Article

The primary role of the article is to emphasize individual identity. It gives distinction to an object of thought. Robertson says, "The article is associated with gesture and aids in pointing out like an index finger."[4] The article focuses attention on a particular person or thing. When the article is used, the object is unquestionably definite; when it is not used, the object may or may not be definite. In English the article is used only with substantives, but in Greek it is used also with infinitives, adverbs, phrases, clauses, or even with entire sentences. "The use of the article with the phrase, clause, or sentence specifies in a particular way the fact expressed: marks it out as a single identity."[5]

Often an important interpretation turns on the significance of the article. In Luke 18: 13 the publican, by his use of the article, identifies himself as *the* sinner. The American Standard and even the Revised Standard follow the King James in rendering the articular noun by "a sinner" (but the American Standard does have "the sinner" in the margin). The point of the penitent's prayer is largely missed unless we note the article. "He seemed to himself to be the great sinner· of the

---

[4]R, p. 756.
[5]D-M, p. 137 f.

world as did Paul later (I Tim. 1:15)."⁶ Williams renders the petition, " 'O God, have mercy on me, the sinner!' " and Montgomery, " 'O God, be merciful to me, the sinner!' "

The article may denote previous reference. This is called the anaphoric use (from *ana*, again, plus *pherō*, to carry), and refers to the repetition of a word or phrase at the beginning of successive clauses. Anaphora may be illustrated by many examples in the New Testament. For the use of the article with the second mention of a word, see "magi" of Matthew 2:1, but "the magi" in verse 7; "living water" in John 4:10, but "the living water" in verse 11; "sepulcher" in John 19:41, but "the sepulcher" twice in 20:1. See also Revelation 15:1, 6.

An awareness of the anaphoric use of the article is a great help to the interpreter. Note that in Revelation 12:3 where the seven-headed, ten-horned monster is introduced, he is called *a* great red dragon (the article not used), whereas in every subsequent reference to him in the Revelation he is called *the* dragon (the article used), indicating that there is but one such dragon set forth in the Apocalypse. Therefore the dragon of chapter 20 and that of chapter 12 are identical. Notice how fully the description of him in the two chapters agree. In chapter 12 he is said to have "seven heads and ten horns, and seven crowns upon his heads. And his tail drew the third part of the stars of heaven, and did cast them to the earth" (vss. 3-4). It would be most unreasonable to contend for a literal interpretation of these verses, but logical to take them as symbolic. Since the dragon of chapter 12 is not literal, and inasmuch as he is the same monster described in chapter 20, we conclude that the dragon of chapter 20 cannot be a literal creature, but is symbolic.

In Mark 9:23, in the Nestle text, we have an anaphoric use of the article. The father of an afflicted boy had brought his son to Jesus and said, "If thou canst do anything, have compassion on us and help us." Jesus uses the article to refer to the father's "if" clause, to point out the man's lack of faith, and to challenge him to perfect trust. Jesus says: "As to your statement, If thou canst! All things are possible to him who believes!" The meaning of the passage is brought out by a number of translations,

---

⁶RSG, p. 70.

including American Standard, Moffatt, Goodspeed, Weymouth, Williams, Montgomery, Revised Standard, J. B. Phillips.

In Galatians 3:23 the thought of the Greek is lost in the rendering "before faith came" (King James, Englishman's, Godbey, American Standard, Revised Standard and others). Such a rendering infers that faith was not exercised prior to the coming of the Christ. But we know that God had many people of faith in Old Testament times. Paul says, "Abraham believed God" (Gal. 3:6), and there were many other examples of faith during the pre-Christian era. Galatians 3:23 is another illustration of the anaphoric use of the article. Paul says, "Before the coming of *the faith* [*tēn pistin*] we were kept locked up under law." *The faith* refers to the particular faith previously defined in the context (vs. 22). This faith was made possible by the historic appearance of the Redeemer. Paul thus draws a distinction between faith in the general sense, and faith in the specific sense in Jesus Christ. In Galatians 3:23, English Revised has "the faith" in the margin. Confraternity has "the faith," and Montgomery "the Faith." Way says, "before the advent of this faith," and "before this faith came" is the rendering of Moffatt, Goodspeed, Williams. In verse 25 *faith* is articular in the Greek, again referring to verse 22.

In James 2:14 the anaphoric function of the article is significant. The rendering, "Can faith save him?" (King James, Englishman's, Berry, Goodspeed, and others) implies that a person is not saved by faith. But justification by faith is one of the cardinal doctrines of the New Testament. In the first part of verse 14 James inquires, "What does it profit, my brothers, if anyone says he has *faith* [*pistin*, anarthrous], but does not have works?" Then he asks, "*The faith* [*hē pistis*, articular] is not able to save him, is it?" The article with the second use of the term faith (*the faith*) designates the particular faith previously mentioned in the verse, i.e., the non-works-producing sort of faith. So James is saying that genuine faith demonstrates its existence with works. Follow his delineation through the rest of the chapter (James 2:15-26). Among the translations which bring out the force of the Greek idiom in 2:14 are English Revised, "Can that faith save him?"; Weymouth, Montgomery, "Can such faith save him?"; and Williams, "Such faith cannot save him, can it?"

The article may be used in the generic sense to denote a representative of a class. By this means one class is distinguished from all others and identified by certain characteristics. Note, "The overseer must be irreproachable" (I Tim. 3:2); "the heathen and the publican" (Matt. 18:17); "the workman is worthy of his wages" (Luke 10:7); "the foxes have lairs, and the birds of heaven nests" (Matt. 8:20; Luke 9:58). Other examples of the generic use include "rock" and "sand" (Matt. 7:24-26).

The article is used with abstract nouns to make them definite and specific. Dana and Mantey have pointed out that abstract nouns are usually general in character and application, and therefore indefinite; but when it is desired to apply the sense of an abstract noun in some special and distinct way the article is placed with it. For example, in the New Testament, *grace* (without the article) denotes favor as an abstract attitude or the gracious character of God in general.[7] But when Paul says, "Indeed by *the grace* [articular] you are in a state of having been saved [perfect tense] through faith" (Eph. 2:8), the article specifies the grace of God in its particular application for believers in the atonement of Christ.

Likewise *alētheia* (without the article) is *truth* in a general sense—that which is in conformity with reality—but *hē alētheia, the truth,* restricts the application and gives it a particular emphasis. In the New Testament *the truth* means the message of the gospel, the revelation of God in Jesus Christ. Therefore, a person's attitude toward the gospel is a matter of life or death. Everyone who hears the message must take an attitude, either of receptivity and faith, or of rejection and unbelief (Mark 16:16). Paul shows the importance of receiving the love of the truth in order to be saved (II Thess. 2:10). Any other course leads to eternal tragedy. Refusal to humble one's heart and open one's mind to the truth of the gospel leaves the life a prey to all sorts of moral delusions. Thus it is that some people believe a lie, thinking it is truth, and are lost (cf. vss. 11-12).

The article distinguishes the subject of a sentence from the predicate. It is a general rule that the term with the article is the subject, whatever the word order may be. Thus we have,

---

[7]D-M, pp. 141, 142.

"the Word was God" (John 1:1); *"the Word* became flesh"
(vs. 14); *"God* [articular] is spirit" (4:24); *"God* [articular]
is love" (I John 4:8); *"God* [articular] is my witness" (Rom.
1:9); *"the last* shall be first, and *the first* last" (Matt. 20:16).

In a passage like John 1:1, important theological implications
are reflected in the syntax of the article. John's expression, "The
Logos [Word] was God," is very significant. If the article were
used also with *theos* (God), the statement would mean that
all of God was expressed in the Logos. As it is, the Logos is not
"a God" nor equated with the sum total of God. The other
persons of the Trinity are implied in *theos*. The Christian doctrine of the Trinity is that Jesus Christ the Son is *theos* (God),
but not *ho theos*, that is, the Son is not the whole Godhead.

When the article occurs with both the subject and the predicate, they are identical and interchangeable. Illustrations are
plentiful. *"The field* is *the world"* (Matt. 13:38); *"the life* was
the light" (John 1:4); *"the sting* of death is *the sin,* and *the
power* of the sin is *the law"* (I Cor. 15:56). "If the subject is
a proper name, or a personal or demonstrative pronoun, it may
be anarthrous while the predicate has the article (Cf. Jn. 6:51;
Ac. 4:11; I Jn. 4:15)."[8]

The Article with Nouns Connected by "Kai"

About 1798 Granville Sharp, after examining several thousand examples in Greek, noted the following syntactical principle:

"When the copulative *kai* connects two nouns of the same case [viz.,
nouns (either substantive or adjective, or participle) of personal description respecting office, dignity, affinity, or connection, and attri-
butes, properties, or qualities, good or ill], if the article *ho* or any of its
cases precedes the first of the said nouns or participles and is not repeated before the second noun or participle, the latter always relates to
the same person that is expressed or described by the first noun or participle: i.e., it denotes a farther description of the first named person." [9]

Regarding the foregoing rule, Robertson says, "Sharp stands
vindicated after all the dust has settled."[10] Dana and Mantey
say, "The rule by Granville Sharp of a century back still

[8]D-M, p. 149.
[9]A. T. Robertson, *The Minister and His Greek New Testament,* p. 62.
[10]*Ibid.,* p. 66.

proves to be true."[11] There are many illustrations of this rule in the New Testament. Compare "pastors and teachers" (Eph. 4:11), where the terms refer to the same persons but indicate different functions. In other words, pastors are also teachers. Compare same idiom in II Peter 1:1 where Jesus Christ is described as "our God and Savior"; 2:20 where he is called "the Lord and Savior"; and Titus 2:13 where he is called "our great God and Savior." Thus the Greek article plays an important role in setting forth the deity of Jesus Christ.

Anarthrous Construction

The use of the article denotes identity, while the anarthrous construction (nonuse of the article) emphasizes character or quality. "Sometimes with a noun which the context proves to be definite the article is not used. This places stress upon the qualitative aspect of the noun rather than its mere identity."[12] For example, "righteousness of God" (Rom. 1:17) means the God-kind of righteousness. Taking it as the ablative case, it indicates the righteousness which has its source or origin in God. As the genitive case it describes the righteousness as inherent in God's character. In Mark 11:22, Jesus says *Echete pistin theou,* which could be objective genitive, "Have faith in God"; or subjective genitive, "Have the faith of God" (the God-kind of faith). Such faith has its source in God, is a divinely imparted faith, being engendered in the believer by the Holy Spirit (cf. I Cor. 12:9; Eph. 2:8).

Anarthrous predicate expressions like "God is spirit" (John 4:24), "God is love" (I John 4:8) are significant. They reveal what God is in his essential nature. The subject and predicate in such statements are not identical, hence are not convertible. In instances where both subject and predicate have the article, they are interchangeable or convertible. Only then could the meaning be "God is love" or "Love is God." As we have it in I John 4:8, love is an attribute of God. He has other qualities besides love. Compare "the Logos was God" (John 1:1), where the nonuse of the article with *God* stresses the qualitative character of the Logos, indicating that the Logos is divine.

In Romans 1:1, "gospel of God" is anarthrous, showing the

---

[11]D-M, p. 147.
[12]D-M, p. 149.

divine quality of the gospel. Again the ablative idea is that of source or origin, while the genitive would emphasize the gospel as the possession of God. The gospel is the good news of which God is the author. The verbal form would denote the work of proclamation or carrying the gospel, but here the noun indicates the message itself.

In Paul's charge to Timothy, a solemn exhortation which we might call the Apostle's final message to the ministry and church of God, he says, "Do the work of an evangelist" (II Tim. 4:5). The Greek phrase, *ergon poiēson euaggelistou,* is anarthrous, thus emphasizing the qualitative aspect of the preacher's work. Paul is saying, "Let your work be characterized by evangelism." It is clear that soul winning is the pre-eminent task of the ministry. Furthermore, evangelism is the responsibility of the entire church. All Christians are involved in this great endeavor. The purpose of Christ in calling apostles, prophets, evangelists, and shepherds and teachers is "for the equipping[13] of the saints for the work of ministering" (Eph. 4:11-12).

In I Peter 3:1 is another example of the significance of the articular and anarthrous constructions. Peter says that if any husbands obey not *the word,* they may without *a word* be won by the chaste conduct of the wives. *The word* refers to the gospel, while *a word* refers to a spoken plea by the Christian wives. No person is ever brought to Christ without *the word,* inasmuch as saving faith comes by hearing God's word (Rom. 10:17), but husbands who know the way of salvation may without undue discussion be won to the Savior by the godly behavior of the wives.

A prepositional phrase usually implies some idea of quality or kind, and the anarthrous noun is common in such phrases. Thus the expression, "In the beginning" (John 1:1), anarthrous in the Greek, "characterizes Christ as pre-existent, thus defining the nature of his person."[14] The nonuse of the article makes it clear that the Logos, Jesus Christ, is of the character and essence of Deity.

---

[13]This accusative singular substantive is from the verb *katartizō* which often means "to arrange," "put in order," "equip." Polybius uses this verb in the sense of fitting out and equipping fleets for battle.
[14]D-M, p. 150.

The Article and "Law"

Nomos, law, is a term used in the New Testament with a great deal of freedom both with and without the article. It has a wide range of meanings in Paul, especially in Romans and Galatians. A study of this significant word in its various contexts is a most interesting and rewarding effort, as the following examples from Romans show:

1. *Nomos* is common with the article to denote the Mosaic law (Rom. 2:14b, 18, 20, 23b, 26, 27a; 4:15a, 16; 7:4, 5, 6, 7a, c, 12, 14, 16, 22, 23b; 8:3, 4, 7).

2. *Nomos* is also common without the article to denote the Mosaic law (Rom. 2:14a, c, 17, 23a, 25a, b, 27b; 3:31a, b; 4:13, 14; 5:13a, 20; 7:7b, 8, 9, 25a; 9:31; 10:4, 5; 13:8, 10).

3. At least once, articular *nomos* means law in general (Rom. 7:1b), while anarthrous *nomos* is common for law in general (2:13a, b; 3:20a, b, 21a, 27a, 28; 4:15b; 5:13b; 6:14, 15; 7:1a, 2a).

4. *Nomos* with the article means a principle or force of action in Romans 7:21, 23c; 8:2a, b; and without the article it has this meaning in 7:23a, 25b.

5. *Nomos* with the article is used to designate the Scriptures. It means a single statute in Romans 7:2b, 3; the Pentateuch in 3:21b; and the Old Testament in 3:19a, b.

6. *Nomos* with the article means man's moral nature in Romans 2:15; and without the article has the same meaning in 2:14d.

7. *Nomos* without the article means the principle of faith in Romans 3:27b.

As already pointed out in this chapter, the article denotes identity, while the anarthrous construction emphasizes quality or character. In the light of this basic distinction, it seems that where *nomos* represents the Mosaic legislation, the word without the article refers to that legislation not primarily as Mosaic but to its character as law.

The foregoing material is sufficient to show the importance of the Greek article. The careful exegete always gives close attention to this element of syntax, for the use or nonuse of the article is significant for accurate interpretation. An understanding of the nature and function of the article is often a source of light from the Greek New Testament.

Selected Bibliography

A. Texts

New Testament, Septuagint, Fathers

Hē Kainē Diathēkē. Text with critical apparatus. Prepared by Eberhard Nestle. London: British and Foreign Bible Society, 1934.

The New Testament in the Original Greek. The text revised by Brooke Foss Westcott and Fenton John Anthony Hort. New York: The Macmillan Company, 1928.

Novum Testamentum Graece. Cum apparatu critico curavit. D. Eberhard Nestle. Novis curis elaboravit D. Erwin Nestle. Stuttgart: Privilegierte Wurttembergische Bibelanstalt, 1932.

Novum Testamentum Graece et Latine. Apparatu critico Instructum Edidit. By Augustinus Merk S. J. Roma: Sumptibus Pontificii Instituti Biblici, 1944.

Septuaginta Id Est Vetus Testamentum Graece Iuxta LXX Interpretes. Editit Alfred Rahlfs. Stuttgart: Privilegierte Wurttembergische Bibelanstalt. Vols. I, II, 1949.

The Septuagint Version of the Old Testament. With an English translation, and with various readings and critical notes. London: Samuel Bagster and Sons, 1879.

The Old Testament in Greek According to the Septuagint. Edited by Henry Barclay Swete. Cambridge: At the University Press, 1912.

The Apostolic Fathers. With an English translation by Kirsopp Lake. Volume I. Cambridge, Massachusetts: Harvard University Press, 1949.

Literary Koine

The Roman Antiquities of Dionysius of Halicarnassus. With an English translation by Earnest Cary, on the basis of the version of Edward Spelman. Vol. I. Cambridge, Massachusetts: Harvard University Press, 1937.

Josephus. With an English translation by H. St. J. Thackeray. Vol. IV, Jewish Antiquities. Cambridge, Massachusetts: Harvard University Press, 1930.

Josephus. With an English translation by Ralph Marcus. Vol. VI, Jewish Antiquities. Cambridge, Massachusetts: Harvard University Press, 1937.

Lucian. With an English translation by A. M. Harmon. Vol. IV. Cambridge, Massachusetts, Harvard University Press, 1925.

Philo. With an English translation by F. H. Colson and the Rev. G. H. Whitaker. Vol. I. Cambridge, Massachusetts: Harvard University Press, 1929.

Plutarch's Lives. With an English translation by Bernadotte Perrin. Vol. II. Cambridge, Massachusetts: Harvard University Press, 1948.

Polybius: The Histories. With an English translation by W. R. Paton. Vol. I, 1922; III, 1923; IV, 1925. Cambridge, Massachusetts: Harvard University Press.

The Works of Josephus. Vol. III. By William Whiston. New York: Harper and Brothers, 1859.

Papyri, Ostraca, Inscriptions

Davis, W. Hersey, *Greek Papyri of the First Century.* New York and London: Harper and Brothers Publishers, 1933.

Deissmann, Adolf, *Light from the Ancient East.* New York: Harper and Brothers, 1927.

Fayum Towns and Their Papyri. By Bernard P. Grenfell, Arthur S. Hunt, and David G. Hogarth, with a chapter by J. Grafton Milne. London: The Office of the Egypt Exploration Fund, 1900.

Greek Papyri in the Library of Cornell University. Edited with translations and notes by William Linn Westermann and Casper J. Kraemer, Jr. New York: Columbia University Press, 1926.

The Hibeh Papyri. Part I. Edited with translations and notes by Bernard P. Grenfell and Arthur S. Hunt. London: The Offices of the Egypt Exploration Fund, 1906.

Milligan, George, *Here and There Among the Papyri.* New York: George H. Doran Company, n.d.

Michigan Papyri. Vol. V. Papyri from Tebtunis. Part II. By Elinor Mullett Husselman, Arthur E. R. Boak, William F. Edgerton. Ann Arbor: The University of Michigan Press, 1944.

The Oxyrhynchus Papyri. Edited with translations and notes by Bernard P. Grenfell and Arthur S. Hunt. London: The Offices of the Egypt Exploration Fund. Part II, 1899; Part III, 1903; Part XV, 1922. Edited with translations and notes by Arthur S. Hunt: Part VIII, 1911; Part IX, 1912.

Catalogue of the Greek Papyri in the John Rylands Library, Manchester. Vol. II. Edited by J. De M. Johnson, Victor Martin and Arthur S. Hunt. Manchester: The University Press, 1915.

Selections from the Greek Papyri. Edited with translations and notes by George Milligan. Cambridge: At the University Press, 1912.

The Tebtunis Papyri. Part I. Edited by Bernard P. Grenfell, Arthur S. Hunt, and J. Gilbart Smyly. London: Henry Frowde, 1902.

Winter, John Garrett, *Life and Letters in the Papyri.* The Jerome Lectures. Ann Arbor: University of Michigan Press, 1933.

Zenon Papyri. Vol. I. Business papers of the third century B.C., dealing with Palestine and Egypt. Edited with introductions and notes by William Linn Westermann and Elizabeth Sayre Haseneohrl. New York: Columbia University Press, 1934.

Zenon Papyri. Vol. II. Business papers of the third century B.C., dealing with Palestine and Egypt. Edited with introductions and notes by William Linn Westermann, Clinton Walker Keyes, and Herbert Liebesny. New York: Columbia University Press, 1940.

English Translations, New Testament

The English Hexapla. Exhibiting the Six Important English Translations of the New Testament Scriptures, Wycliffe (1380); Tyndale (1534); Cranmer (1539); Genevan (1557); Anglo-Rhemish (1582); Authorized (1611). The original Greek text after Scholz, with the various readings of the Textus Receptus and the principal Constantinopolitan and Alexandrine Manuscripts, and a complete collation of Scholz's text with Griesbach's edition of 1805, preceded by a history of English translations and translators. London: Samuel Bagster and Sons, n.d.

The New Testament of Our Lord and Savior Jesus Christ. Published in 1526, being the first translation from the Greek into English by that eminent scholar and martyr, William Tyndale. Reprinted verbatim, with a memoir of his life and writings by George Offor. London: Samuel Bagster, 1836.

The Holy Scriptures. Faithfully and Truly Translated (Out of Douche and Latyn in to Englishe). By Myles Coverdale, Bishop of Exeter. 1535. London: Samuel Bagster, 1838).

The Sacred Writings of the Apostles and Evangelists of Jesus Christ. Commonly styled the New Testament. Translated from the original Greek by George Campbell, James Macknight and Philip Doddridge, Doctors of the Church of Scotland. Printed and published by Alexander Campbell. Buffaloe, Brooke County, Virginia, 1826.

A Translation of the Gospels. With notes. Two volumes. By Andrews Norton. Boston: Little, Brown and Company, 1856.

The Emphatic Diaglott. Containing the original Greek text according to the recension of J. J. Griesbach. Based on the interlinear translation, on the renderings of eminent critics, and on the various readings of the Vatican Manuscript. With an alphabetical appendix. By Benjamin Wilson. New York: Fowler and Wells Company, Publishers, 1864.

The New Testament. Translated from the Greek text of Tischendorf. By George R. Noyes. Boston: American Unitarian Association, 1870.

The New Testament. Translated from the critical text of Von Tischendorf. With an introduction on the criticism, translation and interpretation of the Book. By Samuel Davidson. London: Henry S. King and Company, 1875.

The New Testament. Translated from the Greek text of Tregelles by Joseph B. Rotherham. Second edition, revised. London: Samuel Bagster and Sons, 1878.

The Gospels, Acts, Epistles and Book of Revelation, Commonly Called the New Testament. A new translation from a revised text of the Greek original. By John Nelson Darby. New edition, revised. New York: Loizeaux Brothers, n.d.

The Syriac New Testament. Translated into English from the Peshitto Version, by James Murdock. Sixth edition. Boston: H. L. Hastings, 1893.

The Englishman's Greek New Testament. Giving the Greek text of Stephens 1550, with the various readings of the editions of Elzevir 1624, Greisbach, Lachmann, Tischendorf, Tregelles, Alford and Wordsworth, together with an interlinear literal translation, and the Authorized Version of 1611. Third edition. London: Samuel Bagster and Sons, Ltd., 1896.

The Interlinear Literal Translation of the Greek New Testament. With a new Greek-English New Testament Lexicon by George Ricker Berry. Chicago: Wilcox and Follett Company, 1897.

The New Testament of Our Lord and Saviour Jesus Christ. Authorized or King James Version of 1611. Cleveland and New York: The World Publishing Company, n.d.

The New Testament of Our Lord and Saviour Jesus Christ. Being the version set forth A.D. 1611 compared with the most ancient authorities and revised A.D. 1881. Oxford: At the University Press, 1881.

The New Testament. American Standard Version, A.D. 1900. New York: Thomas Nelson and Sons, 1901.

The American Bible. The New Testament, five volumes, by Frank Schell Ballentine. Scranton, Pennsylvania: Good News Publishing Company, 1902.

The New Testament, Revised and Translated. By A. S. Worrell. Philadelphia: American Baptist Publication Society, 1904.

The Corrected English New Testament. A revision of the "authorized" version (by Nestle's Resultant Text), prepared with the assistance of eminent scholars, and issued by Samuel Lloyd. London: Samuel Bagster and Sons, Ltd., 1905.

The Twentieth Century New Testament. Revised edition. New York: The Fleming H. Revell Company, 1909.

The New Testament in Modern English. By Ferrar Fenton. New York: Oxford University Press, American Branch, 1919.

Translation of the New Testament from the Original Greek. By Rev. W. B. Godbey. Cincinnati: Office of God's Revivalist, n.d.

The New Testament: A New Translation. By James Moffatt. New York: Harper and Brothers, 1930.

The Riverside New Testament. A translation from the Original Greek into the English of Today. By William G. Ballantine. Boston and New York: Houghton Mifflin Company, 1923.

The New Testament: An American Translation. By Edgar J. Goodspeed. Chicago: The University of Chicago Press, 1942.

The New Testament in Modern English. Centenary Translation. By Helen Barrett Montgomery. Philadelphia: The Judson Press, 1946.

The People's New Covenant (New Testament). Scriptural Writings, translated from the Meta-physical standpoint by Arthur E. Overbury. Monrovia, California: Published and for sale by Arthur E. Overbury, 1925. Didion and Company, New York; and Hyatt and Lyon, Los Angeles, Printers.

The New Testament in Modern Speech. An idiomatic translation into everyday English from the text of the Resultant Greek Testament. By Richard Francis Weymouth. Edited and partly revised by Ernest Hampden-Cook. Pocket edition. Boston: The Pilgrim Press, n.d.

The New Testament in Modern Speech. By Richard Francis Weymouth. Newly revised by James Alexander Robertson. Fifth edition. Boston: The Pilgrim Press, 1932.

The New Testament: A Translation in the Language of the People. By Charles B. Williams. Chicago: Moody Press, 1949.

The Complete Bible. An American Translation. The Old Testament translated by J. M. Powis Smith and a group of scholars; the Apocrypha and the New Testament translated by Edgar J. Goodspeed. Chicago: The University of Chicago Press. 1939.

The New Testament of Our Lord and Savior Jesus Christ. Translated into English from the original Greek by the very Reverend Francis Aloysius Spencer, O.P. Edited by Charles J. Callan, O.P., and John A. McHugh, O.P. New York: The Macmillan Company, 1940.

The New Testament in Basic English. New York: E. P. Dutton and Company, Inc., 1941.

The New Testament of our Lord and Savior Jesus Christ. Translated from the Latin Vulgate. A revision of the Challoner-Rheims Version. Edited by Catholic scholars under the patronage of the Episcopal Committee of the Confraternity of Christian Doctrine. Paterson, New Jersey: St. Anthony Guild Press, 1943.

Berkeley Version of the New Testament. With brief footnotes by Gerrit Verkuyl. Berkeley, California: James J. Gillick and Company, 1945.

The New Testament of Our Lord and Savior Jesus Christ: A New Translation. By R. A. Knox. New York: Sheed and Ward, 1945.

Revised Standard Version of the New Testament. New York: Thomas Nelson and Sons, 1946 and 1952.

The New Testament of Our Lord and Savior Jesus Christ According to the Douay Version. With an introduction and notes by J. P. Arendzen. London: Sheed and Ward, 1947.

Letters to Young Churches. A translation of the New Testament Epistles. By J. B. Phillips. New York: The Macmillan Company, 1951.

The Gospels. Translated into Modern English. By J. B. Phillips. New York: The Macmillan Company, 1953.

The New Testament of Our Lord and Savior Jesus Christ. The Letchworth version, in modern English. By T. F. Ford and R. E. Ford. Letchworth, Hertfordshire: Letchworth Printers, Ltd., 1948.

The Holy Bible. Revised Standard Version. New York: Thomas Nelson and Sons, 1952.

The Letters of St. Paul and Hebrews. Translated by Arthur S. Way. Chicago: Moody Press, 1950.

The New Testament According to the Eastern Text. By George M. Lamsa. Philadelphia: A. J. Holman Company, 1940.

B. Lexicons and Dictionaries

The Analytical Greek Lexicon. Consisting of an alphabetical arrangement of every occurring inflection of every word contained in the Greek New Testament Scriptures. London: Samuel Bagster and Sons, n.d.

Biblico-Theological Lexicon of New Testament Greek. By Hermann Cremer Fourth English edition. Edinburgh: T. and T. Clark, 1895.

The Classic Greek Dictionary. Chicago: Follett Publishing Company, 1949.

A Critical Lexicon and Concordance to the English and Greek New Testament. By Ethelbert W. Bullinger. London: Longmans, Green and Company, 1924.

A Greek-English Lexicon. Compiled by Henry George Liddell and Robert Scott. A new edition revised and augmented throughout by Sir Henry Stuart Jones, with the assistance of Roderick McKenzie, and with the co-operation of many scholars. Vols. I and II. Oxford: At the Clarendon Press, 1940.

A Greek and English Lexicon to the New Testament. By John Parkhurst. London: Printed by Thomas Davison, Whitefriars, 1817.

A Greek-English Lexicon of the New Testament and Other Early Christian Literature. A translation and adaptation of Walter Bauer's Griechisch-Deutsches Worterbuch zu den Schriften des Neuen Testaments und der ubrigen urchristlichen Literatur. Fourth revised and augmented edition, 1952. By William F. Arndt and F. Wilbur Gingrich. Chicago: The University of Chicago Press, 1957.

A Greek and English Lexicon: Originally a Scripture Lexicon; and Now Adapted to the Greek Classics. With a Greek Grammar prefixed. By Greville Ewing. Third edition. Glascow: The University Press, 1827.

A Greek-English Lexicon of the New Testament. Being Grimm's Wilke's Clavis Novi Testamenti. Translated, revised and enlarged by Joseph Henry Thayer. Corrected edition. New York: American Book Company, 1889.

Greek and English Lexicon of the New Testament. By Edward Robinson. A new edition. New York: Harper and Brothers, Publishers, 1850.

Greek Lexicon of the Roman and Byzantine Periods (From 146 B.C. to A.D. 1100). By E. A. Sophocles. New York: Charles Scribner's Sons, 1900.

A Manual Greek Lexicon of the New Testament. By G. Abbott-Smith. Third edition, reprinted. Edinburgh: T. and T. Clark, 1948.

The Vocabulary of the Greek Testament. Illustrated from the Papyri and other nonliterary sources. By James Hope Moulton and George Milligan. London: Hodder and Stoughton, 1914-1929.

C. Concordances

A Complete Concordance to the Holy Scriptures of the Old and New Testaments. By Alexander Cruden. New edition. New York: Fleming H. Revell Company, n.d.

A Concordance to the Greek Testament. According to the texts of Westcott and Hort, Tischendorf and the English Revisers. Edited by W. F. Moulton and A. S. Geden. Second edition. Edinburgh: T. and T. Clark, 1899.

A Concordance of the Hebrew and Chaldee Scriptures. Revised and corrected. By B. Davidson. London: Samuel Bagster and Sons, 1876.

A Concordance to the Septuagint and the Other Greek Versions of the Old Testament. By Edwin Hatch and Henry A. Redpath. Oxford: At the Clarendon Press, Vols. I and II, 1897; III, 1906.

The Englishman's Greek Concordance of the New Testament. Ninth edition. London: Samuel Bagster and Sons, Ltd., 1903.

The Exhaustive Concordance of the Bible. By James Strong. Eleventh printing. New York: The Methodist Book Concern, 1940.

A Handy Concordance of the Septuagint. Giving various readings from Codices
    Vaticanus, Alexandrinus, Sinaiticus, and Ephraemi; with an appendix of
    words, from Origen's Hexapla, etc., not found in the above manuscripts. Lon-
    don: S. Bagster and Sons, Ltd., 1887.

D. Commentaries

Abingdon Bible Commentary. New York: 1939.
Clarke's Commentary. Volumes V and VI. Nashville: Abingdon Press.
Critical and Exegetical Handbooks. By Heinrich August Wilhelm Meyer. New
    York: Funk and Wagnalls. Gospel of Matthew, 1884; Acts of the Apostles, 1886;
    Epistle to the Romans, 1884; Epistles to the Corinthians, 1884.
The New Testament of Our Lord and Saviour Jesus Christ. The text in the Author-
    ized Translation, with A Commentary and Critical Notes. By Adam Clarke. A
    new edition, condensed and supplemented from the best modern authorities by
    Daniel Curry. New York: The Methodist Book Concern, n.d.
The Greek Testament. By Henry Alford. London: Rivingtons: Vols. I, 1874; III,
    1871; IV, 1875. Boston: Lee and Shephard: Volume II, 1878.
The Expositor's Greek Testament. Edited by the Rev. W. Robertson Nicoll. Five
    volumes. Grand Rapids, Michigan: Wm. B. Eerdmans Publishing Company, n.d.
International Critical Commentary. New York: Charles Scribner's Sons. Willoughby
    C. Allen, *The Gospel According to Matthew,* 1907; Rev. Ezra P. Gould, *The
    Gospel According to St. Mark,* 1903; the most Rev. and right Hon. J. H. Ber-
    nard, *The Gospel According to St. John,* Vol. II, 1929; the right Rev. Archibald
    Robertson and the Rev. Alfred Plummer, *First Epistle of St. Paul to the Co-
    rinthians.* Second edition, 1916; T. K. Abbott, *Epistles to the Ephesians and to
    the Colossians,* 1902.
Commentary on the New Testament. The Interpretations of R. C. H. Lenski. Co-
    lumbus, Ohio: The Wartburg Press. 1934-1946.
The Preacher's Homiletic Commentary. New York: Funk and Wagnalls Company,
    n.d.
The Pulpit Commentary. Edited by the Very Rev. H. D. M. Spence and by the Rev.
    Joseph S. Exell, M.A. Grand Rapids: Wm. B. Eerdmans Publishing Company,
    1950.
Westminster Commentary on the Acts of the Apostles. An exposition by Richard
    Belward Rackham. London: Methuen and Company, 1901.
Word Pictures in the New Testament. By Archibald Thomas Robertson. Six vol-
    umes. Nashville: Broadman Press.

E. Greek Grammars

Bevier, Louis, *Brief Greek Syntax.* New York: American Book Company, 1903.
Goodwin, William W., *Greek Grammar.* Revised by Charles Burton Gulick. Boston:
    Ginn and Company, 1930.
Hadley, James, *A Greek Grammar for Schools and Colleges.* New York: D. Apple-
    ton and Company, 1887.
Harrison, Gessner, *A Treatise on the Greek Prepositions and on the Cases of Nouns
    with Which These Are Used.* Philadelphia: J. B. Lippincott and Company, 1858.
Jannaris, A. N., *An Historical Greek Grammar.* London: Macmillan and Company,
    Ltd., 1897.
Jelf, William Edward, *A Grammar of the Greek Language.* Vol. II, Syntax. Oxford
    and London: John Henry and James Parker, 1861.
Smyth, Herbert Weir, *A Greek Grammar for Schools and Colleges.* New York:
    American Book Company, 1916.
Thackeray, Henry St. John, *A Grammar of the Old Testament in Greek According
    to the Septuagint.* Cambridge: University Press, 1909.
Thumb, Albert, *Handbook of the Modern Greek Vernacular.* Edinburgh: T. and T.
    Clark, 1912.

F. New Testament Greek Grammars

Blass, Friedrich, *Grammar of New Testament Greek.* Translated by Henry St. John
    Thackeray. London: Macmillan and Company, Ltd., 1898.
Burton, Ernest DeWitt, *Syntax of the Moods and Tenses in New Testament Greek.*
    Chicago: The University of Chicago Press, tenth impression, 1930.
Buttmann, Alexander, *A Grammar of New Testament Greek.* Andover: Warren F.
    Draper, Publishers, 1873.
Chamberlain, William Douglas, *An Exegetical Grammar of the Greek New Testa-
    ment.* New York: The Macmillan Company, 1954.

Dana, H. E., and Julius R. Mantey, *A Manual Grammar of the Greek New Testament.* New York: The Macmillan Company, 1957.

Davis, William Hersey, *Beginner's Grammar of the Greek New Testament.* New York and London: Harper and Brothers, Publishers, 1923.

Green, Samuel G., *A Brief Introduction to New Testament Greek.* Fourth edition. London: The Religious Tract Society, n.d.

Huddilston, John Homer, *Essentials of New Testament Greek.* New York: The Macmillan Company, 1937.

Machen, J. Gresham, *New Testament Greek for Beginners.* New York: The Macmillan Company, 1932.

Moulton, James Hope, *A Grammar of New Testament Greek.* Vol. I, Prolegomena. Edinburgh: T. and T. Clark, 1906.

Moulton, James Hope, *An Introduction to the Study of New Testament Greek.* Fourth edition, revised. London: Charles H. Kelly, 1914.

Nunn, Rev. H. P. V., *A Short Syntax of New Testament Greek.* Cambridge: The University Press, 1913.

Robertson, A. T., *A Short Grammar of the Greek New Testament.* New York: Harper and Brothers, 1908. Sixth edition, 1923.

Robertson, A. T., *A Grammar of the Greek New Testament in the Light of Historical Research.* Fifth edition. New York: Harper and Brothers, Publishers, 1931.

Robertson, A. T., and W. Hersey Davis, *A New Short Grammar of the Greek New Testament.* New York: Harper and Brothers, 1931.

Vine, W. E., *New Testament Greek Grammar.* London: Pickering and Inglis, 1930.

Webster, William, *The Syntax and Synonyms of the Greek Testament.* London: Rivingtons, Waterloo Place and High Street, Oxford, 1864.

Winer, George Benedict, *A Grammar of the Idiom of the New Testament.* Seventh edition, enlarged and improved by Dr. Gottlieb Lunemann. Andover: Warren F. Draper, 1892.

Winer, George Benedict, *A Treatise on the Grammar of New Testament Greek.* Translated from the German by W. F. Moulton. Third edition revised. Edinburgh: T. and T. Clark, 1882.

G. Books

Cobern, Camden M., *The New Archeological Discoveries and Their Bearing upon the New Testament and upon the Life and Times of the Primitive Church.* New York: Funk and Wagnalls, 1921.

Conybeare, F. C., and St. George Stock, *Selections from the Septuagint According to the Text of Swete.* New York: Ginn and Company, 1905.

Dana, H. E., and L. M. Sipes, *A Manual of Ecclesiology.* Kansas City, Kansas: Central Seminary Press, 1944.

Deissmann, Adolf, *Bible Studies.* Authorized translation, incorporating Dr. Deissmann's most recent changes and additions by Alexander Grieve. Edinburgh: T. and T. Clark, 1901.

Deissmann, Adolf, *New Light on the New Testament from Records of the Graeco-Roman Period.* Translated from the author's manuscript by Lionel R. M. Strachan. Edinburgh: T. and T. Clark, 1907.

Deissmann, Adolf, *The New Testament in the Light of Modern Research.* The Haskell Lectures, 1929. Garden City, New York: Doubleday, Doran and Company, Inc., 1929.

Giles, P., *A Short Manual of Comparative Philology for Classical Students.* Second edition, revised. London: Macmillan and Company, Ltd., 1901.

Girdlestone, Robert Baker, *Synonyms of the Old Testament.* Grand Rapids: Wm. B. Eerdmans Publishing Company, 1948.

Goodspeed, Edgar J., *Problems of New Testament Translation.* Chicago: University of Chicago Press, 1945.

Grant, Frederick C., *An Introduction to New Testament Thought.* New York: Abingdon-Cokesbury Press, 1950.

Heitmuller, Wilhelm, *Im Namen Jesu.* Gottingen: Vandenhoeck and Ruprecht, 1903.

Kennedy, H. A. A., *Sources of New Testament Greek, or The Influence of the Septuagint on the Vocabulary of the New Testament.* Edinburgh: T. and T. Clark, 1895.

Leete, Frederick D., *New Testament Windows.* New York: Funk and Wagnalls Company, 1939.

Mantey, Julius R., *Was Peter a Pope?* Chicago: Moody Press, 1949.

Moule, Handley C. G., *The Epistle to the Romans.* London: Pickering and Inglis Ltd., n.d.

Robertson, A. T., *The Minister and His Greek New Testament.* New York: Harper and Brothers, 1923.

Simcox, William Henry, *The Language of the New Testament.* London: Hodder and Stoughton, 1889.

Swete, Henry Barclay, *An Introduction to the Old Testament in Greek*. Cambridge: At the University Press, 1914.
Trench, Richard Chenevix, *Synonyms of the New Testament*. Grand Rapids, Michigan: Wm. B. Eerdmans Publishing Company, 1948.
Wuest, Kenneth S., *The Practical Use of the Greek New Testament*. Chicago: Moody Press, 1946.
Wuest, Kenneth S., *Studies in the Vocabulary of the Greek New Testament for the English Reader*. Grand Rapids, Michigan: Wm. B. Eerdmans Publishing Company, 1946.

H. Periodical Articles

Badcock, F. J., "Baptism for the Dead," *The Expository Times*, LIV (1943), 330.
Blakeney, E. H., *"Huper* with Genitive in New Testament," *The Expository Times*, LV (1944), 306.
Bruce, F. F., "Baptism for the Dead," *The Expository Times*, LV (1944), 110-11.
Dayton, Wilber T., "John 20:23; Matthew 16:19 and 18:18 in the Light of the Greek Perfect Tenses," *The Asbury Seminarian*, II (1947), 74-89.
Deissmann, Adolf, "The Philology of the Greek Bible: Its Present and Future," *The Expositor*, seventh series, IV (1907). "I. The Greek Bible as a Compact Unity. The New Linguistic Records," 289-302. "II. The Problem of 'Biblical' Greek," 425-35. "III. Septuagint Philology," 506-20.
Deissmann, Adolf, "The Philology of the Greek Bible: Its Present and Future." "IV. New Testament Philology," *The Expositor*, seventh series, V (1908), 61-75.
Heawood, Percy J., "Baptism for the Dead," *The Expository Times*, LV (1944), 278.
Kennedy, Rev. H. A. A., "Two Exegetical Notes on St. Paul. I. A Special Use of *en*," *The Expository Times*, XXVIII (1917), 322-23.
Mantey, J. R., "Unusual Meanings for Prepositions in the Greek New Testament," *The Expositor*, XXV (1923), 453-60.
Mantey, J. R., "The Causal Use of *Eis* in the New Testament," *Journal of Biblical Literature*, LXX, Part I (1951), 45-48.
Martin, H. V., "Baptism for the Dead," *The Expository Times*, LIV (1943), 192-93.
Moulton, James Hope, "Some New Subjects of Theological Study," *The Expositor*, seventh series, IX (1910), 73-85.
Moulton, James Hope, and George Milligan, "Lexical Notes from the Papyri," *The Expositor*, seventh series, V (1908), 170-85; 262-77; VI (1908), 84-93.
Thomson, J. Ramsay, "Baptism for the Dead," *The Expository Times*, LV (1943), 54.
Williams, C. S. C., "Baptism for the Dead," *The Expository Times*, LV (1944), 110.

I. Unpublished Materials

Allen, J. P., "The Force of Prepositions in Compound Verbs in the Perfect Tense in John's Gospel and Epistles." Unpublished Doctor's dissertation, Southern Baptist Theological Seminary, Louisville, Kentucky, 1940.
Blackwelder, Boyce W., "The Causal Use of Prepositions in the Greek New Testament." Unpublished Doctor's dissertation, Northern Baptist Theological Seminary, Chicago, Illinois, 1951.
Cooper, David Lipscomb, "The Use of *En* and *Eis* in the New Testament and the Contemporaneous Nonliterary Papyri." Unpublished Doctor's dissertation, Southern Baptist Theological Seminary, Louisville, Kentucky, 1930.
Dayton, Wilber T., "The Greek Perfect Tense in Relation to John 20:23, Matthew 16:19 and 18:18." Unpublished Doctor's dissertation, Northern Baptist Theological Seminary, Chicago, Illinois, 1945.
Enns, George Marlan, "Baptism for the Dead." Unpublished Bachelor of Divinity thesis, Northern Baptist Theological Seminary, Chicago, Illinois, 1947.
Kendall, William Frederick, "Paul's Use of *Anti* and *Huper*." Unpublished Doctor's dissertation, Southern Baptist Theological Seminary, Louisville, Kentucky, 1935.
Southern, Paul, "The New Testament Use of the Preposition *Kata* with Special Reference to Its Distributive Aspects." Unpublished Doctor's dissertation, Southern Baptist Theological Seminary, Louisville, Kentucky, 1948.

Index of Scripture References

Index of Greek Words